D1473156

BECOMING

Debbie:
I know our God
has His hand on
you and yours.
Know your God
delights in you!
♡ Tammy

TAMMY EVEVARD

BECOMING

THE WOMAN
GOD MADE YOU
TO BE

SERVANT
BOOKS

PUBLISHED BY ST. ANTHONY MESSENGER PRESS
CINCINNATI, OHIO

Unless otherwise noted, Scripture passages have been taken from the *Revised Standard Version*, Catholic edition. Copyright 1946, 1952, 1971 by the Division of Christian Education of the National Council of Churches of Christ in the USA. Used by permission. All rights reserved. Scripture passage marked *NLT* has been taken from *Holy Bible,* New Living Translation, copyright © 1996 by Tyndale Charitable Trust. All rights reserved. Scripture passages marked *NAB* are taken from the *New American Bible with Revised New Testament and Revised Psalms* © 1991, 1986, 1970 Confraternity of Christian Doctrine, Washington, D.C. and are used by permission of the copyright owner. All Rights Reserved. No part of the *New American Bible* may be reproduced in any form without permission in writing from the copyright owner. Quotes are taken from the English translation of the *Catechism of the Catholic Church* for the United States of America (indicated as *CCC*), 2nd ed. Copyright 1997 by United States Catholic Conference—Libreria Editrice Vaticana.

Cover and book design by Mark Sullivan
Cover image © Monica Stevenson Photography | Veer

LIBRARY OF CONGRESS CATALOGING-IN-PUBLICATION DATA
Evevard, Tammy.
Becoming : the woman God made you to be / Tammy Evevard.
p. cm.
Includes bibliographical references (p.   ).
ISBN 978-0-86716-998-0 (alk. paper)
1. Catholic women—Religious life. 2. Women—Religious aspects—Catholic Church. I. Title.
BX2353.E94 2011
248.8'43—dc23
2011021541

ISBN 978-0-86716-998-0

Copyright © 2011, Tammy Boyle Evevard. All rights reserved.

Published by Servant Books,
an imprint of St. Anthony Messenger Press.
28 W. Liberty St.
Cincinnati, OH 45202
www.AmericanCatholic.org
www.ServantBooks.org

Printed in the United States of America
Printed on acid-free paper

11 12 13 14 15 5 4 3 2 1

To the two women who have been my best friends
for as long as I can recall:
my sisters, Joleen Boyle Schanzenbach
and Donielle Boyle Nyland.

C O N T E N T S

ACKNOWLEDGMENTS

To my mom and dad—thanks for bringing me up in a home that was filled with love, laughter, and ice cream, and for being the first ones to share with me the beauty of a God who is bigger than I could ever have imagined.

To my husband Mark—through this journey of many steps we have tripped and stumbled and loved and laughed together. I hope for many more miles with you. This book never would have happened without your support and love (and, of course, your ability to cook dinner or order pizza).

To my children, Patrick, Lauren, and Stephen—you are the greatest joy of my heart, and I am blessed to be your mom; I wish you could see how my heart overflows because of you. Know that the best of what I am today is because of you.

To Anne Marie Cribbin—you are the very best kind of friend: one who loves unconditionally, challenges unapologetically, passionately loves God, has the most amazing wit and humor, loves glitter as much as I do, laughs without reserve, and astounds me with your cooking. You have been the greatest surprise friendship of my life.

To the women who have loved me, challenged me, prayed for me, and been sturdy shelters in the midst of the storms—I am grateful for each of you and what you have brought, and continue to bring, to my life.

To my editor, Kathy Deering—I had *no idea* how important you would be to me! You have been a strong hand guiding me through this process and helping transfer all the many jumbled thoughts and ideas I have onto paper. Thank you.

And, always, to the One who gave me life and calls me into His love—You have stolen my heart and I am changed.

INTRODUCTION

I can't help it. Whenever I'm with a group of women I look at their shoes. Not to compare or critique, but because it says a lot about who they are. How different we are! I see heels and flats, sneakers and hiking boots, knee-high boots and sandals, sparkly shoes and black ones. I love it because it is a simple, yet stunning, reminder of God's amazing creativity and love.

In the fourth chapter of Joshua, God asks Joshua to build a pile of stones as a memorial to all God had done for them while they were on their journey. God had done many things for them, including parting the sea for Joshua and his people (as he had done for Moses). So Joshua and the others of his clan built a large pile of stones to remind themselves of all the good God had done for them.

We need to create piles of stones too, reminders of all God has done in our lives and in the lives of those around us. Memorials of love. Memorials of grace. Many of the stories you will read in this book are other people's stones … and I am blessed they allowed me to tell their stories. These are stories of great perseverance and pain, stories of great love and anguish, stories of great sin and great freedom—and they are the stories that we all can tell. They are our stones, reminders of God's presence in our lives. Even at the most difficult moments, we can look at those stones and remember.

My prayer is that this book will come at just the right moment for you. I want your heart to beat with new joy, refreshed by the reminder of who you are. I hope to enable you to see yourself a little clearer in the mirror as the fog of the world gets wiped away unexpectedly by the hand of your astoundingly creative God. I hope you will be able to see yourself a little more as the woman you were made to be, an amazing creation of a remarkable and loving God.

This book is my pile of stones—maybe more like a pile of shoes—a heartfelt reminder of all the good God brings and the fire we bring to the world.

If you are what you should be,
you will set the whole world ablaze.

—St. Catherine of Siena[1]

CHAPTER ONE

A Love Story

It was the hottest part of the day. The sun beat down on the hardened ground, and each step raised swirls of dust, which choked the air and covered everything. The woman slowly walked down the path, carrying her empty water jar, head bowed and eyes downcast. Myriad complaints ran through her head as she walked: *I don't need anyone.... Who do they think they are, talking behind my back!... I wish I could get out of this town....* She saw the well, and her footsteps quickened.

She had just set her jar down and had begun to haul the bucket up from the bottom of the well when she heard a voice. A man on the other side of the well asked her for a drink. She stood for a moment, frozen in place. A man? Asking her for a drink? Who was this man, and why would he be at the well in the middle of the day?

She moved around to his side of the well and saw him sitting on the ground, leaning against the stones. He looked tired, and for a moment she felt compassion for him. But then all the old pent-up feelings flooded her, feelings of being betrayed by men, ridiculed, kicked out of her homes, abandoned, and looked upon as nothing more than chattel. Her mouth hardened in a thin line and her heart grew cold. She stood up straight and asked him, "How is it that you, a Jew, ask a drink of me, a woman of Samaria?" (John 4:9).

The man said to her, "If you knew the gift of God and who it is that is saying to you, 'Give me a drink,' you would have asked him and he would have given you living water" (John 4:10). Something within her began to break open, something she had not felt in a long time, maybe ever. And thus began one of the most beautiful and profound conversations that Jesus ever had with anyone during his time on earth.

What began as a simple request for water became a discussion about true thirst. What began as another day in the life of this rejected and abandoned woman became a day of freedom that she could never have imagined. Jesus even answered questions that had long burned in her heart, such as where Samaritans should worship. Her heart and her sin, in equal measure, were revealed.

Scholars have theorized that the woman turned the discussion to questions about where to worship to distract Jesus from her history. But others believe that she asked those questions because *she really wanted to know* if God heard her when she went to pray. The Jewish people had always told Samaritans that, for God to hear them, they must worship in Jerusalem. For someone like this woman, Jerusalem was impossibly far away. Her heart cried out to be heard. Jesus didn't dismiss her questions; he answered them, and his answers encouraged her that she was indeed being heard.

We can hardly imagine what this woman's life must have been like in her village. A woman who had lived with five different husbands and who was now living with a sixth man—we cannot begin to fathom her daily life. Women had so little power in those days, and they had to rely almost solely on men to care for them. Yet men with merely a word could divorce their wives for something as simple as an inability to cook or as selfish as not being able to bear children.

We do not know this woman's story. Was she barren, so man after man left her? Was she a home-wrecker, always going after another woman's husband because somehow it made her feel more valued?

I don't think her story is what really matters. What matters is that she was a woman whose village had rejected her; she had made poor choices in her life, and poor choices had been thrust upon her. What truly matters is that this woman would be one of the *most unexpected* people for Jesus to have such a conversation with.

This was no ordinary conversation. Talking to this unlikely woman, Jesus revealed himself, for the first time, as the Savior of the world! No one else knew this yet. And he shared it with *this* woman?

This conversation is also the longest personal conversation with Jesus recorded in all of the Gospels. With this woman? Really? You would think that if Jesus really wanted his word to be spread, he would have picked a mover and shaker of the day, wouldn't you? One of the well-respected men, someone who could command an audience. Or one of the religious leaders. But a rejected woman, a Samaritan, an adulteress?

Isn't that just like God? Over and over he chooses the weakest or most broken to change the world. He chose Moses to lead an entire people out of slavery into freedom, and who was he? A murderer and a fugitive. He chose Paul to write over half of the books of the New Testament and to tell the world about the power of Jesus Christ, and who was he? An accomplice to murder, who looked on while Stephen was stoned to death, and a persecutor of the new Church. God chose Rahab, a prostitute, to help the Israelites by hiding their spies, even at the threat of death (see Joshua 2).

It is just like Jesus to choose the least. So he chose her. We don't even know her name! But Jesus treated her with such great dignity—he saw her as she had been created; he saw her as having purpose and value.

A few minutes of conversation with Jesus radically changed this woman! As their conversation concluded, she abandoned her jar, turned, and ran back along the same path by which she had just dragged her feet. Now she practically skipped into town, shouting out to everybody, "Come and see this man!"

And they did come. That fact is equally remarkable. This woman who had tried to hide as she went to the well at noon, when no one else would be there, now ran and cried out to everyone she saw to follow her back to the well. "Come, see a man who told me everything I have done. Can this be the Christ?" (John 4:29).

At first you might think that "everything" means how Jesus exposed her sin to her. But I think "everything" means so much more. He showed her that her prayers had been heard; he showed her that the Savior had come, and that it was in fact *that very Savior* who spoke to her. Most of all, I think he showed her hope. This was what gave her the ability to fly into town and beckon her fellow villagers to follow her without reserve or fear.

They came in droves. And Scripture tells us that many of the townspeople began to believe—*because of the woman's words* (see John 4:39). In those days a woman's voice was not one of authority or power; the words of a mere woman were not respected. But that day they were. Why? It could be that she just wouldn't stop shouting about it or that she told someone more respected in town and he got them to go. But I don't buy that. I think Jesus knew exactly what he was doing. He chose the smallest, the weakest, to speak his words of grace to a needy town.

I can't help but think that those townspeople were more than a little curious when they saw such a difference in the woman. Of course they wanted to go see this man who had caused such a radical transformation in her. By the end of the account, the townspeople told the woman, "We no longer believe because of your word; for we have heard for ourselves, and we know that this is truly the savior of the world" (John 4:42, *NAB).* The first evangelist announcing the Savior's presence in the world was a woman, a broken woman. Isn't that just like God?

Essential Feminism

Stories like this confirm my belief that I am a feminist—in the strongest sense of the word. You might gasp with surprise to hear me, a conservative Catholic woman, say that. But let me say it again: *I am a feminist!* And I think I'm in pretty good company because I'm confident that Jesus recognizes the true value and dignity of women, as does Pope John Paul II, who said, "In fact, woman has a genius all her own, which is vitally essential to both society and the Church."[1] This is what the true essence of feminism is: seeing that what each woman brings to the world has value and purpose—that women are *vital to the world.*

Jesus himself treated women with tremendous dignity and friendship —unheard of in that culture. It remains much needed in our culture today. While we have much more "freedom" than women in those days—we can go after any career we want, care for ourselves financially, and pursue many goals—we have sacrificed much for this. Seeking equality, we have far too often found only narrowness.

We become narrow when we believe that the only way we can be successful is to imitate men. Jesus did not ask the Samaritan woman or the woman caught in adultery or Mary Magdalene or even his own mother to become manlike in order to be respected or treated with the dignity they deserved. He accepted them as they were and engaged them in their femininity.

What we see around us described as feminism is often an angry masculinization of women.[2] This creates mimicry, not equality. Why, to be considered equal, should we somehow conform to masculinity? At the core of this lie is the idea that we are not enough as we are, as women. This is no better than the women who do not see that they have value outside the home. These are the women who let motherhood define them or, as one woman I know said, "My identity comes from my husband." All of these ideas are skewed. Pope John Paul II, in "The Genius of Women," stated:

> Equality between man and woman is a fact asserted from the first page of the Bible in the stupendous narrative of creation. The Book of Genesis says: "God created man in his own image, in the image of God he created him; male and female he created them" (Genesis 1:27). In these brief lines we see the profound reason for man's grandeur; he bears the image of God imprinted on him! This is true to the same degree for male and female, both marked with the Creator's imprint.[3]

The Creator's "imprint" upon us is an indelible mark that cannot be washed away by choices or hurts or anything else that may happen. Nothing, absolutely nothing, takes away that imprint of the Creator upon our hearts!

When a woman reduces herself to something other than what she was created to be, not only does that individual woman suffer, but our entire society suffers. We see the results of this every day, when women see a child or a pregnancy as an inconvenience that can be easily disposed of, or when women pursue acceptance in a man's world by acting more like men than like women.

I have a friend who works for a Christian organization. The last time I saw her, she had dyed her beautiful, naturally blonde hair red. I asked her why, and she told me that it was because "blondes aren't taken seriously." How sad! Even in a Christian workplace she didn't feel that she was seen as an equal participant in the work of the ministry. She felt she had to compromise to be respected or seen as valuable.

We have reduced ourselves to try to find ourselves. And we have lost.

Insecure at the Core

All of this reduction creates a tremendous feeling of insecurity and uncertainty. In his book *The Tender Heart: Conquering Your Insecurity*, Joseph Nowinsk writes about this uncertainty:

> Insecurity refers to a profound sense of self-doubt—a deep feeling of uncertainty about our basic worth and our place in the world. Insecurity is associated with chronic self-consciousness, along with chronic lack of confidence in ourselves and anxiety about our relationships. The insecure man or woman lives in constant fear of rejection and a deep uncertainty about whether his or her own feelings and desires are legitimate.[4]

This insecurity causes us to lose track of who we were created to be and the very real role that we play in the world.

Spending our lives in the trap of insecurity means that it is virtually impossible for us to offer the world our gifts. We become inert, neutralized, afraid that what we offer is weak and useless. The best seller *The Beauty Myth* explains how the idea of insecurity has affected every part of our lives as women:

> During the past decade women breached the power structure; meanwhile, eating disorders rose exponentially and cosmetic surgery became the fastest growing medical specialty. During the past five years...thirty-three thousand American women told researchers that they would rather lose ten to fifteen pounds than achieve any other goal. More women have more money and power and scope and legal recognition than we have ever had before; but in terms of how we feel about ourselves physically, we may actually be worse off than our unliberated grandmothers. Recent research consistently shows that *inside the majority of the West's controlled, attractive, successful, working women, there is a secret "underlife" poisoning our freedom; infused with notions of beauty, it is a dark vein of self hatred, physical obsessions, terror of aging, and dread of lost control* [emphasis mine].[5]

God himself calls us out of our insecurity, uncertainty, self-hatred, and obsession with our exterior appearance. He calls us his "beloved" (see Song of Songs 2). He calls us his "redeemed" (Isaiah 43), and he tells us that he can never forget us, because we are "carved on the very palm of his hand" (Isaiah 49).

God has called us his own, and if we allow this truth to sink deeply into our hearts, we will find healing. Beth Moore, in her book *So Long, Insecurity*, comments about God's redeeming love: "Although we may have something unhealthy deep inside of us, those in whom Christ dwells also have something deeper. Something whole. Something so infinitely healthy that, if it would but invade the rest of us, we would be healed."[6]

The woman at the well went back into town a new woman. She was now a redeemed woman who had allowed the living water of truth to sink deep and water the dryness of her broken heart. It wasn't just her words that made people listen—it was *she*! I imagine that as she ran back into town, her shoulders were no longer slumped and her head was held high, because she had met *Love*. She was changed, and it showed! She had become whole. She was healed.

Yes, I find great hope in the story of the woman Jesus met at the well. Because if God could use one such as her, then could he not do the same for me and for you?

CHAPTER TWO

Crown of Creation

My favorite Disney movie by far is *Mulan*. The story is a rather typical fairy tale: Someone is being held back from a desire and resorts to fighting, cheating, or lying to achieve the desire, and somewhere along the way a boy and a girl fall in love. But *Mulan* is a bit different for me. It's true that the heroine wants to help her family by fighting in the war and does so by impersonating a man, and she does fall in love with the captain of the army, but there is something far more profound in this story for me.

At the end of the movie, Mulan is brought before the emperor of China, and all assume that she will be imprisoned at best, executed at worst, for her behavior. But the emperor surprises everyone. He kneels before her and says, "You have saved us all."

It gets me every time. In China a woman had no power or rights; she was seen as little more than property. But this man, the emperor himself, saw the beauty of Mulan. And for all the world to see, he knelt before that beauty, not in adoration or worship but in honor. He honored Mulan for all that she had done to try to save both her family and her country.

It's a beautiful picture of a woman being the woman she was made to be, even when it seems to go against all that seems "right." It also gives unspoken credit to God for his amazing creativity. Why would we ever think that God would make us all cookie-cutter images of each other?

In the very first book of the Bible, Genesis, we find the account of how God created the world out of nothing. He created the earth, wind, sea and sky, plants and animals, rocks, and trees. After each new creation, he stepped back to look at what he had just made and said, "This is good" (see Genesis 1).

As his final act, God created humans in his own image and likeness. When God created the parents of the human race as a reflection of his own image, he did not just create a superior model of animal. He made us *different* from all other creatures, because each person, male or female, has a *spirit* that is like his Spirit.

When God looked at that couple he had just created, he said, "This is very good" (see Genesis 1:31). Did you catch that? The man and the woman had done absolutely *nothing* yet. All they had done was to have been *brought into existence*. They stood in God's presence without any expectations to offer him or the world. Without having accomplished anything at all, they were declared "very good" simply because they had been created by God. They were *that* good.

We humans are created in God's image and likeness, and he has never changed his mind about us. We have absolutely everything within us to be the men and women he made us to be. And that is very, very good. *We* are very, very good.

I don't want to argue about how we were created or how we all evolved or when it all happened. My focus is God's place in our creation. God intervened, and we became like him. At some point God's breath was breathed into us (see Genesis 2:7), and we became human.

As women we are part of that creation, part of that "good" God talks about. In fact, the only time during Creation that God did not say that something was good was when he said, "It is not good for man to be alone"—and so he created woman (see Genesis 2:18). We are complete as male and female, and *that* is good!

Woman—the final creation in God's masterpiece of creation. No wonder Pope John Paul II so often referred to the man and woman that God created in his final Genesis act as "the crown of creation"![1] Women are like the finishing strokes of vibrant color on a masterpiece, the all-important details that bring life to the work of art.

Somewhere along the way, we lost sight of the gift of "good" we bring to the world simply by being God's creation. I don't think we wanted to lose sight; I think we just forgot. We forgot that what other people think of us or say about us doesn't change us. We forgot that our beauty can't be measured by pounds, wrinkles, hairstyles, or clothing. We forgot that our value is determined by the same endlessly creative One who created the earth, wind, sea, sky, rainbows, mountains, sunsets, and snow; whose knowledge of beauty is greater than we can imagine and whose expressions of love to the world are more than we can fathom.

He made *you*. And then he said, without hesitation or second-guessing, "This is very good." That statement remains true no matter what life circumstances come your way.

Sold Out

I met Laura (not her real name) at a conference when she was in high school. I was one of the speakers, and she was part of the leadership team that weekend. I spent a lot of time hanging out with this group of teens. Years later, when I asked Laura how she got connected to such a group in the midst of the situation I later found out she endured at home, she told me that she was very good at living various lives. You will be amazed, as I was, at the grasp God had on Laura's heart from the very start.

All of our hearts cry out for love, acceptance, and belonging, and Laura is no different. But while many of us lose track of the fundamental truth that we have intrinsic value in God's eyes, Laura was not willing to let that truth go. Here is one small part of her journey, in her own words:

> Years of sexual abuse and mental anguish left me desperate for answers. Who was I? Did I matter? These were my heart cries. Sold for sex at the age of six by my own mother, I was sure of the lies I had been spoon-fed. I was "dirty" and "bad," and God did not love me. How could he, so beautiful, love me? My mind taunted me with that often.

But somehow, deep in my heart, my spirit testified to the real truth: I am the daughter of the King, and he is my warrior Daddy. He wants to see me fly and soar, not be bound in chains, mute from lies.

I was far away from that life, the life I had been made to live in fear and obedience. I was attending college; I was finding healing; God was building my heart anew. And then my mother, Susan [not her real name], showed up. My little-girl heart screamed at her as she invaded my place of peace and healing, at the same time begging her to love me. From the first time she had dropped me off at a man's house when I was six, she had stated, "If you love me, you will do this." What little girl isn't desperate for her mother's approval and affection? How I sought after that!

I went to dinner with her. At the dinner, she said she had someone she wanted me to meet. And if I loved her, I'd be nice. He walked in. He introduced himself as Mike [not his real name] and laughed as he said, "And you, my dear, are nothing but a prostitute, yes?"

Do I agree with him? Do I affirm what I always had thought was true? Or could I trust that God had a big enough plan of redemption for me? Could I really walk away from what I've known into the unknown? Isn't the unknown terrifying to a heart so used to bondage?

It was hard to leave that restaurant. I finally learned the idea of walking by faith, of allowing Truth to sustain you when the world cannot. Before I stood up from that white linen-covered table, I smiled the most genuine smile I have ever allowed a man like that to see, and certainly my own biological mother too. I smiled because I knew that even if I failed at everything else in my life, I would succeed in one thing today. I would walk away, and Jesus would hold me in his arms and tell me that nothing else matters.

As I smiled, they grinned too. Maybe they hoped I'd agree quietly and forget any shred of dignity I may have possessed. Instead I opened my mouth and simply declared, "I am leaving."

It was rather fitting to end my relationship with Susan on that note. Her parting shot was, "It's that Jesus thing, isn't it? Don't you get that he doesn't care?" Usually I called her Susan to her face, but for this one moment, I decided to call her the name of which she should have been worthy.

"No, Mom, he does care. That's why I'm leaving. Jesus loves me.... And if I stay here, Mike here is going to kill any hope I have left. He will kill me, and you don't care. Jesus cares. He loves me, and I am leaving believing that."

I left on shaky legs but standing on firm ground. Truth had a grasp on my heart and soul, and I was walking toward freedom.

Laura called me the day after this dinner episode. I cried with her— tears of joy at her courage and strength. I was so proud of her that day. She had made so many strides toward freedom, but that evening at the restaurant, she took a giant leap. In all the darkest places, Laura never lost sight of who she was in Christ.

Today Laura is a college graduate who works with young women who have been sexually abused or sold into prostitution, sharing with others the freedom that comes through Christ, a freedom that she has experienced firsthand. Laura, more than most people I know, could relate to the idea of having been yoked into slavery—and choosing *not* to be. Ever. Again. "For freedom Christ set us free; stand fast therefore, and do not submit again to a yoke of slavery" (Galatians 5:1).

Too Many Toothpastes

In spite of the fact that most of us do not have to cope with situations as horrific as Laura's, it seems to me that we are surrounded with a never-ending dissatisfaction—on every level. You can never be too thin, too young-looking, too powerful in your job, too famous in your work, too in shape, too trendy, too hip, too rich, or too fashionable. You can never have teeth that are too white.

Seriously—have you seen how many toothpaste brands are out there? You could have a nervous breakdown just trying to find the "right" toothpaste so that your teeth are not only super healthy but also super white! There are really only a few ingredients in toothpaste, so why all the craziness about which kind to buy?

I admit I've done it myself: I've bought various brands thinking, hoping, wishing they would whiten all my Diet Coke stains while making my teeth super strong too! If the purchase of toothpaste, as simple as *that* is, has become such a ridiculous situation, what about the things that matter more? My faith, for instance. My health. My job. My boyfriend or husband (or lack of either).

You can probably look at another woman and tell her that she is beautiful, made in God's image, and loved by him. And you probably believe it. But if I asked you to say those same words to yourself as you looked in the mirror, you would probably feel awkward and struggle to say them. You would struggle even more to *believe* them.

You've forgotten how God sees you. The world around you screams so loudly, "Never, ever be satisfied! Always look for another way to change yourself. Never, *ever* believe that you are already good enough."

We all forget. We forget the truth that has been written in the very core of our being. Hear these words of truth from the *Catechism of the Catholic Church*: "The dignity of the human person is *rooted in his creation in the image and likeness of God*" (CCC, #1700, emphasis mine).

Rooted! God's image is imprinted deep within us, and it can't be erased or washed off. It's a root, and it's our very life. Without a root a plant dies. Without the root of God's creation, we don't exist. And when we forget that truth—that we are, at the very core of our being, made in God's image and likeness—we get lost. Lost in dissatisfaction, self-loathing, selfishness, materialism, obsession with exercise, eating disorders, depression, addictions, abusive or manipulative relationships, promiscuity....

If we're not careful, one day we will have forgotten completely *whose* we are. To be brutally honest, this is just what Satan, the evil one, wants! "For we are not contending against flesh and blood, but against the principalities, against the powers, against the world rulers of this present darkness, against the spiritual hosts of wickedness in the heavenly places" (Ephesians 6:12). There is a genuine battle for our hearts and our spirits, to make us lose sight of who we are, to place our identity in our exterior, to essentially become non-women, no longer true to our distinctive selves.

As women we have a role in the world that cannot be replaced by men. We bring life and love to the world around us, because, by the very way in which we are made, we are "life bearers." Yet giving birth to children is only one of the ways that this gift expresses itself in our lives.

Women are the heart of the world. We offer a place of welcome; we carry a nurturing hospitality that men do not possess. And I'm not talking about if we can cook or have a clean house or know how to throw a good party. It's deeper than that. We offer a vital and important part of the world that encompasses a nurturing, welcoming, and intuitive role. We are a necessary and valuable part of humankind. We are equal to men, with the same dignity, the same value. But the beauty of creation is that we bring different gifts to the world. "I do not understand," Mother Teresa said, "why some people are saying that women and men are exactly the same, and are denying the beautiful differences between men and women. All God's gifts are good, but they are not all the same."[2]

When you get caught up in dissatisfaction with yourself, you can no longer bring life to the world. Immersed in a completely self-centered way of life, you are unable to see beyond what is wrong with you. No longer can you appreciate your uniqueness and celebrate who you were created to be; the real you gets covered up and lost.

Women are powerful, although Satan wants us to think we are weak. (Just ask a woman who has given birth—there is no wimpiness involved!) Women are strong, although Satan wants us to think that we are fragile and even broken. Women are beautiful, although Satan wants us to think that we are never beautiful enough. A woman is the crown of God's creation, but Satan will do everything in his power to convince us that we are an afterthought. And even the very best of us can get caught in his lies.

True Freedom

It was Christmas Eve, and I was cooking. I'm not really a cook at all. But on Christmas Eve our tradition is to make homemade pizza. Well, I can at least do that. I was out in the kitchen making a wide range of pizzas with all kinds of toppings and different cheeses, pretending I was a good cook.

That year my parents, sister, and brother had all come to have Christmas with us. My sister Donielle came into the kitchen and stood silently next to me, watching what I was doing. Soon she asked me if I could put less cheese, no meat, and less sauce on her pizza.

I looked over at my sister, standing there with not an ounce of fat on her. She could use a little cheese and maybe some meat, I thought. Everything my sister did had to do with being skinny. She ate very little and exercised fanatically. She was trapped by an ideal she couldn't live up to, and it had become an obsession. She felt lost. Dissatisfied. Nothing was good enough. Blinded to the beautiful woman she was, she was literally starving herself to death.

I am glad to say that, shortly after this Christmas incident, Donielle got some help and became (and has remained) a healthy, beautiful woman who celebrates life with scoops of ice cream! Later, reflecting on her experience, Donielle said, "I think eating disorders are an epidemic in our society based on a culture we have created that *values the physical versus the spiritual.* To me an eating disorder is a physical reaction to the self-starvation that we have inflicted on ourselves. Food becomes the enemy, and food is what our body and mind become obsessed with."

Satan would love nothing more than our death, both physical and spiritual. I hated watching my sister go through that addiction, pain, and struggle as Satan dug in his claws, grabbed her insecurities, and tried to convince her how weak and insufficient she was. Satan is a deceiver, and those are all lies straight from the very pit of hell. Lies!

To underline this point when I was speaking to a group of young women, I had them shout out, "We're not gonna take it!" as loudly as they could. It made them all laugh, but then they stood up and shouted it a bit louder. And then we talked about how we really could choose not to take it any longer. No longer would we accept that we are not enough as we are and spend all our time and energy "fixing" those things. No longer would we buy into the idea that we are "toys" for men with all our "enhancements" and Barbie-doll look-alike attempts. No longer would we believe that our exteriors are what matter most.

This deception starts young. Recently I was with three thirteen-year-olds who told me that they were "fat." As I looked at them, I saw three young women who were definitely not overweight, although they did not happen to have the skeletal look of many of their friends. They hated that they had a bit of curve in their bellies and hips and that they had breasts already. In other words, they had begun to hate the women they were becoming.

It is with the onset of puberty that eating obsessions typically start, with starving, binging, and purging. The desire to stay as slim as possible for as long as possible becomes the goal. It makes me sad for the women of our generation and their daughters.

Our culture has a narrow view of beauty. A fast-growing trend in high-school graduation gifts is breast enlargement. Too many of us attempt to look like supermodels, but we can't compete with air-brushed images.

I recently attended a conference with a thousand teen girls. The speaker asked everyone in the audience who struggled with an eating disorder to stand so that we could pray with them. I almost fell over as I watched more than 50 percent of the women in that room stand up. It wasn't just the teens—it was their chaperones, their youth ministers, and their mothers. I stood in the back of that room with tears running down my face as I looked at what Satan had done. He is convincing us to literally, *physically*, kill ourselves. We are made for much, much more, and we are meant for much, much better than this.

Psalm 139 has a beautiful description of the amazing way God sees us. My favorite verse states, "Wonderful are your works" (verse 14). For years I've talked to women about how we are "wonders" of creation. (And I don't mean what a priest friend of mine often says to me when he hears me talk about this scripture: "Oh, Tammy, I *do* wonder about you....")

If God's works are wonderful, and if God made me, doesn't that make me wonderful, too? *Wonder*ful. I pasted a sticky note in the front of my Bible that says, "I am a Wonder." It's been there for years, and I've never stopped saying this to myself and to others. We are wonders of an amazing God who loves us more than we can measure.

No, we're *not* gonna take it. Not anymore. It's time to stand up and acknowledge that we are made for something better. Regardless of where you have been, what you have chosen or not chosen to do, you can *never* change the fact that you were made in God's image and that he loves you completely and passionately, beyond your imagination. Of course you don't deserve it; we have all fallen into sin, made poor choices, and not lived as the people he has created us to be. But at the end of the day, there is nothing, *nothing at all*, that can separate us from the love of God (see Romans 8:38–39).

So the next time you look in the mirror and begin to criticize yourself, remember that the face you are so unhappy with or the body that you are so disappointed in was made *by* God and *in the image of* God. The divine image is present in every single person (see *CCC,* #1702). Made in God's image, we are his. He has never let go of us, and he never will. We remain wonders of God's amazing creation!

Beloved

Once upon a time, in a land far, far away, a beautiful baby princess was born. Her parents adored her and named her Beloved. They gave her their love and clothed her in beautiful dresses.

As the princess grew into a young girl, she learned how to ride horses and braid her hair, and she ate beautiful and tasty foods. When the princess became a teenager, she learned how to dance and paint and play the harp. The princess was very, very happy, and the king and queen loved her very much.

One day the princess went for a long walk in the wonderful forest near her home. It was a lovely day, and she picked some wildflowers to take home. Continuing on her way, she tripped over a log and hit her head on a rock. When the princess woke up, she had no recollection of who she was. She looked down and saw that she was wearing a beautiful dress, but she could not remember where she was from.

The princess got up and began running out of the woods, desperately trying to find out who and where she was. She came to the edge of the forest and saw a little hut with trash piled up all around it. An old woman was leaning over a fire, making some kind of soup. The princess went up to the woman and asked, "Do you know who I am?"

The woman looked at her, recognized her as the princess, but said to her, "You are a peasant girl who lives with me here."

The princess looked down again at her beautiful dress, and the old woman said, "That dress was stolen from the castle—it doesn't belong to you. Let me go get your clothing."

The woman brought out a pile of smelly rags and gave them to the princess to wear. The princess took off the beautiful gown, put on the rags, and began to do the chores the woman demanded that she do. She ate weak soup and lived in a trash heap of a hut. She spent months and months like this, believing she was a peasant girl and never looking for her castle. As time went on, her hands became calloused from the hard labor, she was often sick from the lack of nutrition, and more often than not, she cried herself to sleep.

One day, from afar, she saw a procession and ran to the edge of the forest to see who it was. It was the king and queen! Wanting to get a closer look, she found herself at the front of the crowd. As the king and queen passed by, she stared in awe at their magnificence.

As they glanced over at her, the king's face filled with shock, and the queen's face crumpled into tears. Abruptly the king commanded the driver to stop the carriage, and he asked the girl to come over to him. The girl was frightened as she hesitantly walked over to the carriage. The king asked her name. She told him, "Forgotten." The king asked her if she remembered anything about a castle and horses and painting. Forgotten said she did not, but sometimes she dreamed of such things.

The king then looked her in the eyes and said, "You are my princess, my Beloved, and you are my beautiful daughter. We lost you and thought we would never find you again. We looked for you for months. We were heartbroken. Come home with us—the castle is yours, and we love you."

Forgotten looked at them, then took a step back and said, "No, no, I'm not a princess; I'm a peasant girl, and I must go back to do my chores before my keeper gets angry." The king and queen tried to press her to come with them, but she refused, certain that they were mistaken. How could someone such as she be a princess? She walked sadly back to her hut.

Ah, the paradox of fairy tales! On the one hand, we've all read them, watched the movies, and dreamed about Prince Charming coming to take us away, certain that we were princesses and just didn't know it. Someday the truth would come out, and we would live happily ever after in a castle far, far away. On the other hand, if someone told us we were princesses, would we recognize our own royalty? Would we believe that we were worthy of the title?

While life is certainly not a fairy tale, there are truths we have not yet grasped. One of them is this: We *are* all princesses. It's not about wearing frilly dresses or a tiara. We belong to the greatest King of all—the Father of heaven and earth—and he has made us for good things. We were made to live in joy with him, and yet we take ourselves out of his kingdom and live in trash-filled huts, believing that is all we are worthy of. We've wandered far from the castle, chosen to put on rags of guilt and shame, and begun to believe that we are worthy of nothing more. We have forgotten where we once lived. We fill ourselves with the weak soup of materialism, shallow relationships, addictions, and fear when we could be feasting on joy, love, and grace.

We are meant to live as daughters of the King.

Fairy tales captivate us because the true cry of each of our hearts is to be loved in such a manner, to be found by someone who has been searching for us, to be reminded of who we really are. But that part of the story is not a fairy tale. It's really true! You don't have to leave it in fairy-tale land. Choose to believe it, and begin to live the truth of it. Your King has come to claim you. All you have to do is say yes to him.

Choosing Life

I met Katie (not her real name) when she was in high school. She was one of those energetic girls who was involved in everything and really fun to be around. During her high-school years, we stayed in sporadic contact, and I was always glad to hear from her. When she went off to college, she began to write to me more frequently. She seemed to be struggling, and I could tell there was something weighing on her.

Finally she wrote, "What if I told you something I've never told anyone before?" I knew then that we weren't looking at something simple. Over the next few weeks, piece by piece, Katie finally shared with me what had been weighing so heavily on her heart.

On the night of her senior prom, she had had sex for the first time, with her prom date. They did it in the "heat of the moment," and she didn't think much beyond just that, the moment. She regretted it the next morning and swore that she wouldn't do it again.

I'm sure you can guess where this is headed. She found out about a month later that she was indeed pregnant. All she could think was, *I have so much ahead of me! How could I possibly deal with a child?* In her fear of anyone finding out what a "bad" girl she was, having to confront her parents with the news, not going to college, or missing her senior trip, she chose what she thought at the time was the easiest way out. She had an abortion.

Now, many months later, she was finally telling someone for the first time—and I lived two thousand miles away. She was afraid to tell anyone who might say something to a friend or a family member. She was filled with remorse, shame, guilt, and fear. And it showed. She dropped out of college halfway through her freshman year, developed a full-blown eating disorder (something she had struggled with off and on in high school), and began cutting herself compulsively, all in an effort to try to control the regret that was consuming her.

She worked at healing and forgiving herself, but far too often she would be overcome with such guilt and shame that the only way to make the voices subside was to transfer the pain. She would starve herself so her focus was on her empty belly, or she would cut her arms and her legs with knives, needles, or safety pins to transfer the pain within her to her exterior body.

I've heard that in the military, when soldiers prepare for torture, they are taught to hit themselves with their fists in another part of their body in order to "transfer" the pain to a less painful place. This is kind of what Katie did. She was transferring her deep emotional pain to her body.

Over the past few years, I've watched Katie work hard to come back to herself. It has not been an easy road. She sent me a text message just a few months ago: "It's a long journey, isn't it?" Yes, Katie, it is. There are no shortcuts to healing and wholeness. We've all made choices that have thrown us so far from the castle that we believe rags are all we deserve.

Katie wrote a letter to her unborn baby, whom she named Rachel, which means "one with purity." Here is a portion of that letter:

> I cannot go a day without thinking about you. I am so very sorry for what I have done. You didn't deserve to die because of my selfish actions. I only cared about myself at the time, not you. You came unexpectedly, at the wrong time. I was just starting to live my life. I had so much ahead of me, and I couldn't let that go.... I knew that what I was about to do was wrong, but it was the only option I felt I had, so I went through with it. I had no one else to talk to.... My heart aches for you.

Katie is not unlike many of us. She was a vibrant, active young woman who spent a lot of time involved in church and Christian events—she even went to Washington, D.C., every year to participate in the March for Life! Yet when it came right down to it, her faith was shallow and small, *irrelevant* to the life she was living. She had lived a life of faith on the outside, but on the inside she was living in rags. Katie paid a high price for this. She found herself in such pain from her choices and in such shame that there seemed no way out.

But she has begun to find the way. She has started to see a counselor. Her cutting and her starving have decreased to rare occasions. She has not told her family yet about the abortion, and she's still not sure she ever can. Her story is not tied up with a nice red bow and a perfect ending, because life isn't like that; life is messy.

Yet, we have a God who stands at the castle window and watches for us. He is ready to welcome us home, as the father welcomed the prodigal son who wandered far from home, from the truth of who he was, and from all he had been taught as a young man (see Luke 15). When he finally realized that he was starving (in more ways than one), he recognized that being a servant in his father's home would be better than being in self-exile. He began the long trek home. I can imagine that his glorious clothing had become tattered and covered in pig filth. He probably smelled really, really bad. And I'm sure that he walked very slowly, trying to plan out what to say when he arrived home.

The last words he had said to his father were callous and harsh, about money and wanting to leave this wretched, boring place. These words he was trying to form wouldn't be like that. But before he could plan out his speech, his father saw him from far off and came running toward him!

How undignified for a man of his stature to jump off the porch and *run* as fast as he could to greet someone, but he didn't care. The father couldn't wait to hug his wayward son and welcome him home. He shouted to his staff to get a ring and a robe for his son and kill the fatted calf so they could have a celebration. His son was *home!* I've heard it said that the story should be called "The Running Father" rather than "The Prodigal Son," and I can see why.

What we find in this story, just as we do in many of those fairy tales, is the answer to the deepest cry of our hearts. How we wish someone would love us like that! Wouldn't it be wonderful to be waited for, longed for, run to, and dressed in the finest robes?

But it *is* a true story! That running Father is there for us, too. In the midst of our pains and our choices and our everyday messes—from excesses in spending and eating to insecurity and bitterness, hatred and fear, addictions, and anger—the Father is running to us, looking past all of that and saying, "Welcome home! I've been waiting for you! I've waited to show you your castle once again. See these beautiful gowns—they are yours! Take off those rags of fear! That crown of your creation is here for you to wear! Take off that broken crown of despair! You, my beautiful daughter, are home. And you, yes, you, my beloved, are loved completely and absolutely by me, your Father. Welcome home. You are *so* welcome here."

CHAPTER FOUR

I Hate Kids

I hated kids. No, really, I did. And I'm pretty sure I had good reason to.

In late elementary school, like all of my friends, I began to babysit. And while my friends seemed to like it, the only thing I liked about it was the money I made. Otherwise I was just miserable. If the family had good food and a TV, it was a bonus, but for the most part taking care of kids just frustrated me.

I didn't really even try to be nice. I often sang this horrible ditty to them as they went to bed: "Go to sleep, you little creep, let the monsters come to get you. Frankenstein, Dracula, ah, ha, ha, ha, ha, HA!" In my defense (what little I can maintain), I didn't sing it to children old enough to truly understand (at least I don't *think* so). But still, I know. Not nice.

The summer after ninth grade, I took a full-time babysitting job for two kids in elementary school. They were old enough to entertain themselves to some degree, so it was the most ideal babysitting job I could have, if such a thing were possible. We spent lots of time watching TV, swimming at the pool (I invited dozens of my own friends to come along), and eating all the food in the house. Embarrassingly, the mom left me a note one day asking me not to eat quite so much bread while at her house (I was having a real love affair with cinnamon toast).

After that summer was over, my mom suggested gently that it would probably be a good idea if I didn't babysit anymore. I agreed. Oh, *how* I agreed! I had recently had the *absolute worst* babysitting experience of my life.

A neighbor had recommended me (don't ask me why) to a family several blocks away. Reluctantly I agreed, because my cash was growing low with my summer stint over. I found out after arriving at their house that their child was deaf. If I had known this prior to saying yes, I probably would have said no. (I'm guessing that's why they didn't tell me. Most likely they had trouble getting babysitters.)

The evening began. Within the hour the child began to fuss and cry and stand at the window, apparently looking for his parents. I tried to entertain him from my vast repertoire of ideas. That took about fifteen minutes. Nothing seemed to help. The child just stood at the window whining and fussing for his parents (at least that's what I think he was whining about; I couldn't understand him, since he was really unable to speak).

So there I was, with a child who couldn't speak and couldn't hear, and I didn't know any sign language. As the hours ticked on, I got more and more frustrated. Finally I took him outside and put him in a stroller I found in the garage. It was one of those umbrella strollers—really nothing more than a piece of fabric and a couple small poles. In my defense, it was really, really light and not very sturdy—emphasis on "not sturdy."

We walked around the neighborhood. But no matter how far or how long I walked him in the stroller, he would not stop fussing and crying and whining. I started to lose it. I really didn't start with much patience anyway, and this situation was pushing hard on my final nerve. So I began walking faster. And faster.

Pretty soon I was running down the street. As I came around the corner where his house was, I lost control of the stroller and dumped it over right next to the driveway, where the little boy tumbled onto the pavement and began to cry (or continued to cry, maybe just a little louder).

Just as I dumped the stroller, the parents drove up! I turned every shade of red as I quickly picked up their son and brought him into the house. I gave him to his parents and apologized for the spill they had just witnessed. I tried to explain how he had cried all evening and how I was trying to calm him down by walking. (I'm sure they were wondering how running full speed and dumping the stroller would "calm" him.) I was very embarrassed and felt really awkward. I left in a hurry, breathing a sigh of relief. I walked home that night feeling miserable about what I had done.

That was the final straw for me, and it was the last time I babysat. I figured I just wasn't cut out for it. As time went on, that thought morphed into the idea that I wasn't cut out to be a mom, either. I figured I wouldn't feel any differently about my own child than I felt about the kids I babysat for, especially when I watched my sister Joleen, who was amazingly good with kids. She loved babysitting, had immense amounts of patience, and always thought up fun things for the kids to do. I wasn't anything like that; in fact, I couldn't think of anything I liked less (other than eggplant).

Ten years later I was engaged to be married to Mark, and I was so excited to begin my life with him! We planned our wedding and our life together, talking about all the things that were important to us. One night I mentioned to Mark that I didn't want any children. Mark just looked at me and said, "But we're Catholic!" I shared with him my experience as a teen and told him that I just wasn't cut out for motherhood.

Mark didn't say much else about it that night. In later years I asked him why he didn't argue with me or try to convince me otherwise. He told me that he expected that as time went on, my heart would change. He had far more confidence in me than I did!

We got married and began to settle down in our life together. All of my friends were having babies, and I would visit them and hold their babies. They were really sweet, but I was happy to hand them back to their mothers. I never had any feelings of needing children of my own.

A couple of years went by, and I began to think more about having a child—not so much because I now believed that I was cut out for motherhood, but because I knew that Mark was cut out for fatherhood and that a child was a natural expression of our love as a couple. I started to have moments of openness.

One autumn day I told Mark that I thought I might be open to having a child. One month later—I'm not kidding—I was pregnant. I guess that when God gets an opening, he doesn't hesitate! I didn't have time to second-guess myself or rethink the situation. I was pregnant, and I couldn't back out of it.

I spent a lot of my pregnancy in silent fear that I would be a horrible mom, with visions of Frankenstein in my head. One of my friends told me (later) that she was a bit worried about me, because I never spoke of my baby as a baby but always referred to "It." I defended myself by saying that I didn't know the sex, so what *could* I call it? But she didn't need to worry about me. I worried enough for all of us.

To top it off, pregnancy did not set well with my body. It wasn't that I was on bed rest or sick all the time. In fact, my complaints really were nothing compared to those of many women. But they were my issues, and that made them a big deal for me.

One of several examples: I swelled up like a balloon. My sister Donielle came to visit me, and when I opened the door, she said, "Oh, my gosh! Even your nose is swollen!" Granted, she was very young, so I don't hold it against her (now). I couldn't wear shoes for seven months. I didn't wear my wedding band for my entire pregnancy and for several months after.

Labor was a *whole* other story that I don't have enough pages for. And when labor was over and my baby, Patrick Thomas, came into the world, I can tell you that I felt … nothing. Just exhausted. *Really* exhausted.

Fierce Love

We packed our bags, put Patrick in his brand-new car seat, and went home. For twenty-four hours. Within just that much time, Patrick spiked a fever.

Whenever infants under two weeks old spike a fever, they have to be admitted to the hospital immediately, to make sure that they don't have meningitis. It's scary, because babies that young don't have much ability to fight off sickness, and things can get bad very quickly.

I began to cry. And I continued to cry. All the way to the hospital, all the way to the exam room, where they told me that they would have to do a spinal tap to check for meningitis. Now, I knew what that looked like, because I had been a medical assistant for a few years. I knew that the spinal-tap needle is really long and painful.

The doctor on duty was one of the best doctors I knew, and I was so grateful that he was going to care for Patrick. He suggested I wait outside the room while he did the tap. I sat and cried for my Patrick, who had to go through this horrible test. I cried because he was sick.

I tried to call my parents from the pay phone in the lobby, and all I could get out was "Patrick…," and then I crumpled to the floor, sobbing. Mark grabbed the phone from me to tell my folks what was happening, and they got on a plane that afternoon to be with us. I couldn't do anything but cry.

Patrick seemed to be in the room with the doctor for so long. When I think back to that time, all I see is the large wooden doors that Patrick was crying behind and the brown and tan carpet that I spent most of my time sitting on. Finally the doctor came out and handed me Patrick. I tried to comfort my baby son, but he was so distressed.

The doctor informed us that he was sorry it had taken so long, but he couldn't get the spinal tap to work the first time. Or the second time. Or the third, fourth…. It had taken eight tries for him to do the spinal tap! Eight! And so I cried some more. The doctor told us what I already knew: Patrick would have to be admitted for observation until the results of the tests came back.

We got him settled into his room, where the crib looked like a monster bed with my tiny baby in it. Patrick immediately fell asleep; he was so wiped out from the tests. Our doctor suggested that we go home and grab some clothes and food. All I could do was cry.

As we walked into the house, Mark asked me to join him on the couch to pray. We sat facing a huge picture window, through which the vibrant sun was streaming—in such stark contrast to how I felt. How could the sun be shining when everything in me was screaming?

Mark grabbed my hand and began to pray out loud, asking for God's healing for Patrick, wisdom for the doctors, and I don't even know what else. I wasn't really listening. Inside I was screaming, "Not *my* baby!" I couldn't even begin to think of how to pray. I, who had led thousands of prayers, prayed over hundreds of people, been prayed for innumerable times, could not, for the life of me, think of what to say.

Finally the only words that came to me were, "He was yours first." As soon as those words left my lips, I felt as if someone had taken a bucket of warm oil and poured it over my body. I felt an overwhelming sense of peace and quiet that I had not felt before. It's difficult to even put in words how it felt, because it was so complete. There was nothing left in me that was afraid.

I got up from the couch, made some sandwiches, and packed a bag with clothes to take to the hospital. We went back to the hospital and requested a mattress on the floor so one of us could sleep there at all times. I requested a rocking chair so I could rock Patrick when he was awake. Our prayer had given me the strength and grace to care for him and for myself.

It was a very long five days in that hospital, very long. The doctors ruled out meningitis and could not find anything else that might have caused the fever. Patrick was weak after being sick for so many days. When they finally allowed us to go home, that was a good day. We were all exhausted. I think all three of us slept for three days straight, and my parents too.

Today I am filled with gratitude that Patrick is now nineteen years old and six feet tall and eats like a horse each day. But that experience also did something I never expected. I lost my fear. I was never afraid, not ever again, of what kind of mom I could be. I saw what I was capable of, and I knew that I was going to be just fine. I loved that little boy with a fierceness I did not know I was capable of. I believe God used that situation to allow me to become free in my motherhood.

We all have our fears—fears that we aren't good enough, skilled enough, desirable enough, holy enough, generous enough—but God wants us to lose those fears. He longs for us to live in a place of freedom. He will give us all we need to be the women he has made us to be. As we learn to live more in the Spirit of God, we will find more freedom. God promises that "where the Spirit of the Lord is, there is freedom" (2 Corinthians 3:17).

There have been many other times when I have felt fear or have spent weeks or even months in anxiety. Once my husband's ministry was not able to pay him for several months, and I had just had a baby. Creditors called our house at all hours, and I lived in constant anxiety. There was the time I was fired from a job and accused of things I hadn't done. Lawyers were a part of my life, and I lived in turmoil (more about that later).

Through all those times I learned about freedom. I experienced the chains of anxiety and fear, and when I chose to lean on God, those chains fell off (see Isaiah 52:2). To achieve freedom I had to get on my knees and lay at God's feet the things that brought me fear. Then I had to stand on my feet and believe that I could live in that freedom through the good *and* the bad.

Besides Patrick, I went on to have two more children, Lauren and Stephen, and I can't imagine my life without any of them. Because of them my life is richer and I am a better person. They bring me great joy (and yes, at times, great frustration). I am truly blessed to be called Mom. I am free in God, with the true freedom that can come only from him.

And just for the record, I never sang my kids the "Little Creep" song. Not once.

CHAPTER FIVE

Falling Off the Wall

What am I doing here? I thought as I stepped from the plane and immediately slammed into a wall of intense Haitian heat and humidity. Already I could feel the sweat pooling on my lower back and across my forehead. *WHAT am I doing here?*

I don't think I'm a wimpy person by any means, but I really don't like to get dirty or sweaty unless it is from, say, riding a four-wheeler or a motorcycle, running on the beach only to jump into the ocean—you get the idea. Standing still and sweating profusely is not my idea of fun. And yet there I stood in the sweltering sun without a hint of a breeze, sweating and breathing in the thick, humid air.

To be honest, I really hadn't wanted to go on this trip to Haiti. A friend had invited me several times, and I had always found a good reason not to go. I had too much work or too many family commitments, or I was just too busy to make it happen. But this time I had no excuse. I didn't have a job, and my family was completely supportive, even to the point of financially supporting my trip. I had no more excuses. So I started to pack.

As I prepared for the trip, I found that I was anxious about going. How do you find a sleeping bag that's as thin as a piece of paper (because you really don't need *any* blanket, but you must protect yourself from bugs)? I wasn't especially anxious about getting killed (although many Americans die in Haiti each year), I wasn't overly anxious about the shots I had to get (which were *a lot*, I might add—like six hundred dollars' worth of a lot), nor was I anxious about what food I might be given (do they eat rats?).

No, I was anxious, down in my deepest gut, that my heart would be broken. I was afraid that the poverty, hunger, and depth of despair that I would experience in Haiti would break my heart and I would not be able to put it back together again. I felt a little like Humpty Dumpty as he sat on the wall anticipating that very big fall.

But I had made the commitment, so I boarded the plane. And when I got off, it was the smell I noticed first, the smell of decaying garbage that is piled up all over the streets, three and four feet high. It's the smell of people, too many people to feed or to care for; everyone, absolutely every one of them, is hungry. It is difficult to describe the level of poverty in Haiti. Like the stench in the capital city, the poverty is so overwhelming and so bone-deep, you wonder if recovery could ever be possible.

Between the piles of trash and people everywhere, children run around naked and starving. You can see the hunger not just in their eyes but in their distended bellies and the way they scrounge through the trash looking for anything to eat. All over the city, children are left on their own because their parents can't feed them anymore. Out in the streets at two or three years old, many of them die. One thousand children die of starvation in Haiti every—yes, *every*—day. None of my children go to school with even a thousand children, yet I can't imagine their *entire* school dying every day.

I was overwhelmed. I wanted to cover my mouth and nose—or get back on the plane. But that wasn't an option. All I could do was get started with the work I had come to do.

As it turned out, the time I spent in Haiti was filled with more extraordinary moments than I could ever begin to get onto paper. Words don't do justice to what happened in my heart when I gave my plate of food to a child and then watched him share that single meal with four other children. How do regular words describe working next to one young man on the road, lifting boulders with him for hours on end, and toward the end of the day suddenly looking down and noticing that he had only one shoe?

The week I spent in Haiti revealed a side of me I didn't know existed. I hauled boulders, pushed a wheelbarrow, bathed in a river, slept with bugs on my bed, ate a goat that had been tied outside my bedroom window all week, and jumped off a cliff. I was stronger and braver than I ever thought was possible. "I can do all things in him who strengthens me" (Philippians 4:13).

Celebrating Sweat

But the story that I have to tell you is about what happened on a Sunday morning in a little village, because this is where my Humpty

Dumpty moment began. It was Pentecost Sunday, and we planned to go to the local church with the village residents. One of the villagers told me that there was no priest there; only *once a year* did they have Mass with a priest. Right then it struck me how much I take for granted my ability to receive the Eucharist every day if I so choose. I had to wonder, *What else do I so easily take for granted?* I admit that air-conditioning came to mind.

Early Sunday morning we all got ready. Everyone dressed in their best clothes—I was told that all the women wore dresses out of respect for their community and for their God. As we entered the church, which was nothing more than a large cement box with a few small windows, you could feel the heat begin to roll through the room. The people entered and found spots to sit. I remember thinking that I was glad it would be a short service because there would be no eucharistic prayers and so forth. Soon we could get out of the "sweatbox."

This is where I fell off the wall, tumbling down, breaking all my fragile and wasted ways of thinking. This wasn't just church-to-get-it-over-with. This wasn't just church to fulfill an obligation. This was church because this is where these people found life! This was church that lasted for two and a half hours! This was *church*!

Sitting there in my kindergarten-sized chair, I found myself overcome with joy and tears at the same time. The beautiful, heartfelt worship moved me deeply. All I could think about was how selfish and small we are as we sit in our air-conditioned churches in the United States with a mere fifty-nine minutes of worship—and we can't seem even to sit through that. You see people coming in late during the Gospel reading, leaving before the closing prayer, falling asleep during the homily, looking at their watches, coming up to receive Jesus in the Eucharist with eyes half-closed and a halfhearted Amen.

A few years ago a friend of mine, Kelly, shared with me how he longed for his son to receive his first Communion. The trouble was, his son has Down's syndrome. Evan has very limited language and is usually impossible to understand, even for his parents. But Kelly was determined. He talked with his priest, who encouraged him to do the best he could to teach Evan about the Eucharist. Kelly felt that "if Evan understood that this was something very special, then maybe it was time."

Kelly carefully shared the meaning of the Eucharist with Evan through pictures and words, explaining to him the beauty of Christ's gift, his sacrifice for us. Finally the day came for Evan to receive Jesus for the first time. He came forward and received the Eucharist. Kelly was always afraid that Evan would embarrass him by his behavior, and he had extra concern around the holy gift of the Eucharist. Evan said "Amen" as best he was able. And then, as he began to walk away, he stepped in front of the altar, raised his arms high in the air, and shouted, "YES!" Kelly said later, "I was worried that Evan would not understand the meaning of the consecrated Body of Christ and that he would embarrass me. As it turned out, he was the *only* person in church that really understood. I was embarrassed, because I should have been there with him at the front of the altar, arms out, yelling, 'YES!'"

This same feeling came over me in Haiti. In a tiny village in one of the poorest countries in the world, I found riches beyond compare. In this place I came face-to-face with what an amazing gift faith really is. Faith hasn't changed the circumstances of the Haitians, but it is changing their hearts.

Nothing comes easily in that village. This group of people had just spent six straight days doing hard labor for fourteen hours a day. Yet on this Sunday they took a large chunk of their day to prepare to come to church (many walked for hours to get there), and then spent over two hours singing, praising, listening to Scripture, and reciting the prayers of the Church, only to turn around and walk back home to prepare for another day of fourteen-hour labor.

I had to rethink what it means to worship. How do I really, authentically, and truthfully worship God? I was brought up short by the fact that I really couldn't answer this question. I really *wanted* to worship like these villagers who had found something I didn't have. In the midst of their physical poverty, they had found an amazing gift—a relationship with a God who walked with them through trials and difficulty, a God who was present to them, a God who loved them. They absolutely knew it.

I sat in the back of that cement room where the temperature exceeded a hundred degrees, where I couldn't understand a word of the prayers or the songs—and I was in worship. In that sweatbox, I came into the presence of a God who loved me and wanted me to know it. It didn't matter that my dress was soaking wet. It didn't matter that I couldn't sing along. It only mattered that I was there. Just *there*.

I came back to the States and back to my air-conditioned church and my fifty-nine-minute Mass on Sunday. But I wasn't the same, and I hope I will never be again. I find myself more in awe of the Mass, more quiet as I soak it in. I find that the music isn't what moves me, and the homily isn't what captures my heart. What moves me, what captures me, what calls me to holiness, is *being* there. Really being there.

My heart was broken in Haiti. But it wasn't broken the way I was afraid it would. It was *broken open* to God in a way I'm not sure it ever had been before. All the pieces can't be put back together again, and I don't want them to be.

At Mass I find myself soaking in the moments. Listening to the words of Scripture, singing the songs of worship, hearing the eucharistic prayers, reciting the Creed and the Our Father with the community—and receiving Jesus in the Eucharist with a reverberating Amen. I believe! I believe! Amen, I believe!

Oh, I fell off that wall, and I cried out, with arms held high, "Yes!"

It Changes Me

In the film *Shadowlands*, C.S. Lewis comes back from London to Oxford, where his wife, Joy, is dying of cancer. An Anglican priest says, "I know how hard you've been praying.... God is answering your prayers."

"That's not why I pray," Lewis answers. "I pray because I can't help myself. I pray because I'm helpless. I pray because the need flows out of me all the time, waking and sleeping. It doesn't change God; it changes *me*."[1]

I've prayed a lot in my life. I've prayed for everything you can think of: to pass algebra (I didn't), to have an easy labor (I didn't, in triplicate), to find a good job (sometimes I did; sometimes I didn't), for sick people, for our Church, for elections, for my family, for my friends, for people I didn't even know but someone asked me to pray for. On and on the list could go. Sometimes I would ask myself if God even heard my prayers, if he even paid attention. Why were some of my prayers answered and others weren't?

C.S. Lewis understood. It isn't about someone being healed on this earth or in the next, or about a job being found or lost; it's about *him*. It's about letting God be God and letting him change me during my prayer. He changes me to become a woman who trusts that whatever may happen, I will be OK. The circumstances may remain far from perfect, but I have a perfect God who will walk with me. This is especially apparent when I come face-to-face with fear.

I've met a lot of people in this past couple of years who have been ravaged by the economy. White-collar workers making six-figure incomes now work at retail stores, barely making minimum wage. People have lost their homes or their businesses. Because I had been jobless for over a year, we found ourselves edging toward that second group. It created a lot of fear within me, and I didn't like it.

I knew that "there is no fear in love, but perfect love casts out fear" (1 John 4:18). If God is love, then God is not about fear. Fear is contrary to who he is! I hung on to that. I couldn't always see around or above my fear, but I could feel that small seed of truth inside me.

The truth is that, no matter what, *no matter what*, we are going to be OK. That does not mean I will not lose my job, or your boyfriend won't break up with you, or my wallet won't get stolen, or you won't have to make hard choices that hurt. The outcome is not guaranteed. What is guaranteed is that God himself will walk through it with us. He will not leave us alone, not even for an instant. We belong to him.

We all have our hard times. We all have had our panic-in-the-night episodes. Life sometimes is just plain difficult. A few weeks ago I watched a friend bury her twenty-five-year-old son who died of cancer. My son's friend lost his left hand when he was struck by a train last fall. My mom's best friend died of cancer last summer. I've been fired from jobs I loved, I've dated guys who broke my heart, I've been in friendships that got ugly, I've been afraid for my kids, I've wondered where the next car payment will come from. I've longed for closer friends, more lucrative jobs, easier parenting, and so forth. There is always something better to want.

But life is not guaranteed to be rosy. You can wear rose-colored glasses if you want, but all that means is that everything, including the garbage, looks pink. If that makes you feel good, far be it from me to keep you from having pink-looking garbage.

I believe that God knows me. He knows my name, and he knows my heart (see Isaiah 43:1). He has not come to "fix" everything in my life or to wipe away everything that is bad. Life is what it is. Bad things happen to good people all the time.

God gives no guarantees except one: "I am with you always, to the close of the age" (Matthew 28:20). He has promised never to leave me, never to let me walk alone, no matter what I have to walk through. He has promised to be there. While sometimes I wish I had a fairy godmother who could twinkle away all the ugliness and hurt from my life, I have found that God is more than enough.

He never promised me Prince Charming, but he promised—and gave—me a Savior. He never promised me a fairy godmother, but he promised me a faithful Father. He never promised me a rose garden (do you remember that song from the seventies?), but he promised me a place in heaven. And yes, what I see around me doesn't always look good. Sometimes it just looks like pink garbage.

But only in love has my heart found healing. Only in coming before the One who made me, the One who loves me more than I can imagine, can my heart find rest. And so I pray. I converse with the One who has the ability to bring true freedom to my heart and peace to my spirit.

I pray. I pray because it changes me. I pray because without his love, my life wouldn't make sense. Henri Nouwen expresses it this way: "Long before anyone heard us cry or laugh, we are heard by our God who is all ears for us. Long before any person spoke to us in this world, we are spoken to by the voice of eternal love."[2]

Long before any other words were spoken to us, "You are mine" was spoken to the depths of our hearts. And this is why we pray—to hear that voice again.

More Than Being Irish

I sat in a sandwich shop the other day, chatting with a woman I had recently met through work. We spoke about faith and trusting God and seeing him with us in our darkest times, and we found ourselves saying to each other more than once, "I know what you mean!" We found so much in common in our journeys of faith.

Then she mentioned another person she knew, and she said, "But she's a Catholic, and you know they aren't Christian." She stopped and added, "Oh, I'm sure *some* Catholics are Christians, but she isn't." I don't know why I still find it surprising to hear comments like that, but I do. And every time it hurts my heart.

In my work I meet a lot of people who are faithful Christians, and we find much common ground in our core beliefs about God and who he is in our lives. But often, as soon as the conversation moves toward denominations, the Catholics get raked over the coals as being "un-Christian." I know what they're talking about though. Unfortunately, there are a lot of Catholics who say that they are Catholic in the same way that I say I'm Irish. Being Irish doesn't actually have any *real,* everyday effect on my life—other than once a year when I can say that I deserve to wear the green (which, of course, I do!).

Too many Catholics don't allow their faith to be a part of their everyday lives, their true identity, or their decisions. Maybe once a year at Christmas or Easter, they dress up in their finest clothes and go to Mass because that's what a "good Catholic" should do. What a shame!

It's a shame if faith is nothing more than a big white Bible on your shelf that you got for a wedding gift. It's a shame if faith is nothing more than learning the Our Father or being taught to pray, "Now I lay me down to sleep." It's such a loss to see faith as something as shallow as a holiday. Faith is not an add-on. Our faith isn't worth much unless we *live* it.

Living your faith means being immersed in faith, finding that your very identity, your purpose, and your dreams are all born out of faith. I love my faith. I love celebrating the traditions of my faith—the prayers that are repeated every week in the same order and in the same manner, for example. I know there are people who find such things uninteresting and old-fashioned. But I find the sacred prayers comforting. The fact that these words have been passed down from generation to generation brings life to my own faith journey. Across the world, in every language spoken, the same prayers rise to heaven, and the truth remains: We are in need of great grace, and it can come only from a great God.

I've read lots of books and heard many talks about what it means to pray and live the faith, and I've come to realize that it's different for each person. I spent years feeling guilty because I didn't pray the way my friends or my family did, or I didn't spend a specific amount of time in prayer as others did. I've struggled with expectations and guilt about what I did or didn't want to do regarding prayer.

But at the end of the day, I'm in relationship with a God who loves me, Tammy, as I am and who enables and, yes, challenges me to be the best expression of myself in all that I do. My prayers bring me closer to God and closer to the woman I am called to be.

How do I express my prayers? Is there one superior way? God is so big that our relationship with him takes many forms. He speaks to us through Scripture, the sacraments, good books, friends who share with us, quiet prayer, adoration in the chapel, and an enjoyable meal around the table with good and holy friends. We draw near to him when we teach a religious-education class, help a child with homework, and maybe even write a book.

> Where does prayer come from? ...Scripture speaks sometimes of the soul or the spirit, but most often of the heart (more than a thousand times). According to Scripture, it is the *heart* that prays. (*CCC,* #2562)

> *The heart is the dwelling-place where I am, where I live....* The heart is our hidden center, beyond the grasp of our reason.... The heart is the place of decision.... It is the place of truth.... It is the place of encounter, because as image of God we live in relation: it is the place of covenant. (*CCC,* #2563, emphasis mine)

Prayer comes from the deepest part of me.

I've wasted too many minutes on comparisons and guilt and feelings of inferiority around the issues of prayer and faith. If it is indeed our heart that prays, the very core of our being, can we trust that, if we are open, God himself will guide us in our prayer? Can we believe that through the gifts of Scripture, Church teachings, and the sacraments, we will find our way to true prayer?

I trust and believe that. I am beginning to see that prayer has no beginning and no end; it is a never-ending flow of life-changing grace.

CHAPTER SIX

How Bad Do You Want It?

Recently, while I was looking through Facebook at the antics and activities of my friends and family, I saw something that caught me by surprise. A young man had posted on his wall that he was *well aware* that his ex-girlfriend was engaged and would people *please* stop commenting on it. But then he said the most surprising and beautiful thing: He said that, if he wasn't the man for her, he wished her and her fiancé all the very best.

Wow. I could certainly sense some real pain in the words he wrote, but I also saw a remarkable love. The kind that matters—when what you really want for a person is what is best for him or her, even if this means that it hurts you. In the world today we don't very often see this kind of unselfish love.

It reminded me of another love I've seen. A love that has said things such as, "I came so that they may have life, and have it abundantly" (John 10:10), "Daughter, your faith has made you well;

go in peace" (Mark 5:34), and, "Neither do I condemn you" (John 8:11).

I'm not sure we really understand that kind of love. Facebook Boy shows us a small glimmer of it. So does a mother seeing her child for the first time, a young woman watching a young man kneel before her with a small box in his hand, a child smiling, a friend sitting in a waiting room comforting another who is waiting for a prognosis, a daughter sitting next to her elderly mother who has forgotten her name. Yes, these give us a very small glimpse of this Love.

This is the Love that stood in the gap for us. We can't pay it back. No matter how many goats and lambs and birds get sacrificed, their blood running over the altar instead of *our* blood, it can never suffice. This Love declared, "He has sent me to proclaim release to captives" (Luke 4:18).

This Love walked that long road to Calvary for us, while we stood there and shouted at him and spit at him and mocked the One who walked that road so we didn't have to. This Love healed the blind, made the deaf hear, and cured more illnesses than we can imagine. This Love brought hope to a thirsty woman at a well and forgiveness to a woman cast on the ground, covered in nothing more than her guilt and shame.

This is the Love we so desperately need, the very Love that we rejected from the start and continue to reject today. We don't understand it, so we reject it. My body is your bread? My blood is your drink? Become like a child again? Give away all you have and follow me? "I don't get it," we say. "It's too hard to understand." So we reject it, thus rejecting our very heart, the One who keeps us alive. We say no.

Maybe you haven't exactly verbalized it like that. Maybe you've never said no out loud to God. But haven't you said it more than you'd like to admit? We say no when we choose to cheat on our exam or on our spouse ("Just this once," we say); we say no when we choose to give ourselves to someone we don't love (and who does not love us) because we feel lonely or pressured. We say no when we pick up the bottle, or the razor, or the food, or the needle. We say no when we lie to our family about where we have been or what we have been doing. We say no when we fill our lives with so much activity that we don't have time to hear God. We say no when we let our Bibles collect dust and allow our excuses for missing church or showing up late get lamer and lamer. We say no every time we lie to ourselves that the prison of our addiction, pain, anger, resentment, shame, and guilt is what we deserve. We say no every time our insides cry out for the freedom Christ offers and yet we don't take it.

We say no every time we walk away from the only One who can bring us freedom and truth.

Of course, it's easier to say no. *Yes* can be so complicated. It means change. It means making different choices. It means cleaning up and casting out the old. And that doesn't feel comfortable. So we convince ourselves that our path is set, there is nothing better or different for us, we have made our choices, and we can't go back or get out.

Paul tells us in Ephesians, "For we are God's masterpiece. He has created us anew in Christ Jesus, so we can do the good things he planned for us long ago" (Ephesians 2:10, *NLT*).

Created anew? God's masterpiece? If this is true, then why do we stay in the old? We are God's masterpiece! He has chosen to create us anew, by giving us Jesus, who stood in the gap for our sins. He offers us a life of good things that he planned for us long ago. We have good things to do! Jesus speaks to us about not putting new wine in old wineskins (see Matthew 9:17; Luke 5:37). Is it possible that he just might mean we should stop trying to put good, new things into old ways of thinking and living?

It comes down to this: How bad do you want it?

Break a Little

A few years ago there was a story about a young man named Aron Ralston who was climbing by himself in Utah when his arm got pinned under a boulder. He spent five days stuck in a canyon (this is why the buddy system is *still* a good idea, even after kindergarten) until finally, when he knew that he was going to die if he didn't do something, he cut off his own arm with a dull pocket knife.[1] I don't even like to break a nail, yet this man broke the two bones in his forearm and then sawed on it with that knife until his arm was completely cut off. I get a stomach ache just *thinking* about it.

Shortly after this story came out, a priest friend of mine used it in one of his homilies. He kept repeating the phrase, "How bad do you want it?"

It's a worthwhile question to ask ourselves. How bad do you want to be holy? How bad do you want to be all that God has created you to be? How bad do you want out of the prisons you live in? Enough to cut off your own arm? To cut out sin? To cut out those habits that don't bring you life? To cut off those friendships that take you down the wrong path? To cut out addictions? How bad?

Because it won't be easy. You might have to break a couple of bones. You might have to break up with someone or something; you might have to break your ties with a selfish dream; you might have to break yourself a little.

Do you remember the story of the woman who met Jesus at Simon's home (see Mark 14)? She knelt before Jesus, and she broke open a very expensive alabaster jar of perfumed oil and poured it on Jesus' head. Her extravagant gesture was an outpouring of herself for Jesus. She poured her broken self out of a broken jar and in doing so found freedom and life like she had never known.

The jar she broke was worth a tremendous amount of money; quite possibly it was the most valuable thing she owned. But she was willing to break the jar and use up all that was within it for the only One who had the ability to fill her to overflowing with the freedom she so longed for. She was willing to "cut off her own arm." How bad do *you* want it?

One Brushstroke at a Time

Recently I decided to paint my bathroom. I don't know why—I hate painting. More than anything else, I hate *preparing* to paint. Blue tape and drop cloths, brushes and rollers, stir sticks and the paint itself—and then *lots* of paint remover for the million mistakes that I always make.

This time I told myself, "Hey! My bathroom is small. It won't take much time at all to paint it." I need to start recording myself so that when I say things like that, my other self will smack me in the head and remind me of the truth. Which is—I must be honest—that I don't like doing those kinds of household things. I get frustrated really easily, wish I could quit, and find the whole experience tedious and boring.

But once the tape is up, the drop cloths are down, and you've rolled the roller over that wall one time, you're in. You can't really turn back and say, "Oh, never mind—I don't want that wall to be blue after all." Once you make that first swipe, you've got to finish.

So I painted that bathroom. Then I stepped back to look at it, and I could see that one coat wasn't going to do it (even though the man at the paint store told me that it would *definitely* only take one coat). Now I had to apply another coat, or my bathroom would look horrible. So I did a second coat. What happened? It needed a third coat. I bit my tongue lest the expletives make their way out.

I finally got the third coat done and began to remove the blue tape, excited to see the final result. But it didn't work. The tape hadn't protected the ceiling or the floor or the mirror. There were blobs of paint all over my bathroom, and I had to use a razor, a small paintbrush, and paint remover to get rid of all the unwanted mess. The project extended over more than a week.

Painting (for me, anyway) is a lot like rooting out sin or addiction. You have to make a decision to do it. You have to look at the sin you want out of your life and make a conscious decision to get rid of it. You can't just "hope" your sin will leave, just as I couldn't "hope" that my bathroom would be painted when I woke up in the morning. I had to make a choice to do it. And finish it.

How do you root out sin and addiction? One brush stroke at a time. Each piece of that sin or addiction needs to be seen for what it is and, step-by-step, removed from your life.

I know it's easier said than done—kind of like painting. I look at my small bathroom and think, *Oh, I can do this in a couple of hours, and then look how cute my bathroom will be!* I forget about all the steps from *Oh, I can do this* to *and look how cute!* Lots and lots of steps. Big roller steps and small paintbrush steps. And often it takes more than one coat, more than one try.

Spills Happen

Especially when my three kids were small, it was easy for me to get irritated with the messes they made—and there were a lot of them. It seemed that at every meal an entire glass of liquid or plate of food was spilled. I would get so frustrated! I would fume about it, get mad at the child who spilled, and yell, "I'm always cleaning up after you kids!"

One time when I got especially mad, I went to my bedroom and sat on the bed in order to calm down. For the first time I really looked at my anger, and it made me feel awful. This wasn't loving my kids. And what's more, I was making my kids afraid to make mistakes. I could see it in their eyes.

I didn't really know what to do to change. It felt as if my "short fuse" was ingrained in my personality. But I decided to do something. I started to pray for grace and patience every day, and I made a conscious decision to say every time something was spilled, "Accidents happen." I still found myself screaming inside and often gritting my teeth, but at least the screaming on the outside stopped.

Every time I said those words, "Accidents happen," it reminded me of my promise to myself and God to stop being angry about such things. After a while it became second nature to say those words and simply clean up the mess. Pretty soon my kids stopped staring at me with a panicked look on their faces when they spilled something.

I'm embarrassed now when I look back at how I used to treat my kids. But I am far more grateful than ashamed that God allowed me to see that change needed to happen. I am not perfect, but by God's grace, I am free. Now I hardly ever want to yell when an accident happens.

One of my daughter's friends was visiting a few months ago, and she walked by the coffee table where I was removing the nail polish from Lauren's fingernails. As she walked by, the entire bottle of nail-polish remover spilled. I jumped up, grabbed a towel, and tried to wipe it up, but the table was ruined. The paint had bubbled up and was lumpy, and some spots were bare.

I looked at the girl and told her not to worry, accidents happen. Then I went to my room, shut the door, and jumped up and down for a few minutes because I was so upset. I didn't say anything out loud; I just jumped. That represents a victory. I'm free to love when I don't feel like loving, when it's hard to love—even when my table gets ruined!

God promises us freedom. He promises that we can be free from even the most difficult, most entrenched sins that are in us. He promises that "where the Spirit of the Lord is, there is freedom" (2 Corinthians 3:17).

I have a friend who was addicted to pornography for years. When he finally chose to cut out this sin, there was a lot of "brushstroke" work he had to do. He went through intensive counseling, and he set up accountability measures with his wife and confidants. A year or so into this, when he wasn't quite through the process, he shared with me and others at a dinner party that, even though he wasn't there yet, he believed with everything in him that it was possible to be completely free from this sin. There were some skeptics at the table that night as he shared this with us, but I watched his face, full of hope. Now, a number of years later, I believe, and he believes, that he is truly and completely free from the addiction and even the temptation of pornography.

It's not an easy task to paint the bathroom. It's not an easy task to root out sin. But everything we need is right there: a God who offers us forgiveness when we fall and then doesn't hold it against us (see Psalm 103); our ability to take steps, one at a time, brushstroke by brushstroke. Choosing to say no just one time. And then another time. And when we fall, not giving up but getting back up and deciding to say no one more time. Until one day you no longer have to "make" the decision, because it is now rooted in you.

Through prayer, accountability, and practical decisions (like not going to a bar if you struggle with alcohol, or not having a razor in your room if you struggle with cutting), saying no to sin will become easier each day. That's true freedom.

This is what God promises. I guess it just comes down to one thing: How bad do you want it?

C H A P T E R   S E V E N

The Best Kind of Friendship

Liz was my best friend in high school. She was (and is) an amazing person—carrying a joy that no one else seems to have, with a bright smile and a contagious laugh. While I was insecure during those high school years, she was confident. While I was completely confused about my identity, she was comfortable with herself. She was one of the best things that happened to me in high school, which is surprising because we were so different from each other, and our friendship seemed an unlikely one. Because she was confident and sure of herself, she showed me how to be confident, too. Somehow she saw that I had more inside to give than I ever imagined, and she believed that I could be more than I allowed myself to be.

When I was a senior in high school, for example, I found a short, funky hairstyle that I really wanted to try. However, long hair was the popular look. I thought about it a lot, mostly concerned about what others might say. When I told Liz, she just looked at me and said, "If you want the haircut, get it! *Who cares* what others might say!"

So I got the haircut and loved it. I even got compliments from my classmates (including some cute boys). The compliments didn't matter as much as the fact that I had been encouraged to look within myself rather than to others for validation. I started to learn how to go with my own spirit and heart.

A haircut isn't all that important, but that valuable lesson has served me well in my life. Whenever I feel insecure, intimidated, or unsure of myself, I recall Liz—the way she lived and the way she called me to live. Once again I'm reminded to do what my heart calls me to do, to be the woman I was made to be, not someone else. Once again I refuse to allow myself to be validated *or* minimized by those around me.

Liz offered me the best kind of friendship, one that challenged me to step outside the small self that I had become to the brighter and more "real" me. Without even knowing it, she changed my life. I saw her a few months back, more than twenty-five years after graduating from high school, and I told her the impact she had had on my life. She was surprised, never realizing she could have had that kind of an effect.

No One Like Her

Henri Nouwen, in his book *Life of the Beloved,* says this about friendship: "Deep friendship is a calling forth of each other's chosenness and a mutual affirmation of being precious in God's eyes."[1]

It seems to me that this is what friendship is all about. By the very way we live our lives, we invite others to live theirs and recognize their own amazing gift to the world. If we live authentic lives, we will encourage others to do the same. Friendship challenges us to be better than we are, to be open to the opportunities that come our way, to become holy, and to hear God.

Friendships challenge us to be the women we were made to be; they encourage us to be free within. Our friendships bring us closer to God, and they teach us how to forgive, how to love, and how to be vulnerable. Friendships are a necessary part of being the kind of woman who chases after God's heart. They show us both our weaknesses and our strengths; this is what makes them beautiful. Friendships change our lives.

None of my friends are exactly alike in personality, interests, or lifestyle. My friend Joia is an amazing musician and a mother of four small children who is married to a juggler. My friend Judy is single, a hilarious comedienne who loves to surf the waves in California. My sister Joleen is a nurse and the mother of six children, two of whom have autism. My friend Shannon is a wife, mother, youth minister, author, and speaker; she has held my hand more times than I can count as I have taken my maiden voyage in writing. My sister Donielle is the mother of three young children with a high-level executive job who finds time to do several adventure races a year (and matches me in shopping abilities). My mother is tremendously wise and an amazing artist, and she teaches me to listen. My friend Paul knows my weaknesses and always challenges me to move forward, take chances, and seek my dreams. My friend Anne Marie is a storyteller, youth minister, and amazing cook. She can make me laugh until I cry and then, in the next moment, challenge me with her profound faith. I've watched her handle her mother's journey through cancer with grace, love, grief, and tremendous hope.

Each of my friends brings something beautiful to my life—teaching me, challenging me, and loving me by the way they live their lives. In *Bread for the Journey*, Nouwen states it beautifully:

> No two friends are the same. Each has his or her own gift for us. When we expect one friend to have all we need, we will always be hypercritical, never completely happy with what he or she does have. One friend may offer us affection, another may stimulate our minds, another may strengthen our souls. The more able we are to receive the different gifts our friends have to give us, the more able we will be to offer our own unique but limited gifts. Thus, friendships create a beautiful tapestry of love.[2]

The Art of Makeup

I love makeup. I have always loved makeup. I love the colors, the smells, the textures, the glitter, and the packaging. I love trying on makeup, buying makeup, and putting makeup on other people.

My friend Mary does, too, so it seemed only right that we start a makeup business. Yes, this was one of those pyramid things where the ad says, "I'm making thirty thousand dollars a month, and you can too!" It was, unfortunately, not the last time I allowed myself to join one of these. But makeup is makeup, and we really knew our lip glosses and eyeliners!

The first couple of months were fun. We had several parties and sold quite a bit of product. (I think our natural joy about makeup made it an easy sell.) But as time went on, it became increasingly difficult to maintain our schedules with all the meetings. Then finances became an issue, as we tried to figure out which commissions belonged to whom and how to pay for all of our expenses.

One day, after a particularly frustrating argument, we found ourselves so angry that we could not speak to each other. Mary and I had been friends for years, the kind of friends who talked to each other at least once a day. I sat at home fuming about how wrong Mary was and how mad I was at her. This went on for several days.

Finally, one night I was lying in bed unable to sleep, thinking about the argument. For the first time I asked God to help me with this—and in particular to *please* have Mary see the error of her ways and apologize to me. Because, of course, *I* was not in the wrong.

Somewhere deep inside I heard God say, "Tell her you miss her."

I thought, *What? It's not my fault! Mary is wrong, not me! And why would I tell her I miss her? It doesn't even make sense!*

Again, I heard the words, "Tell her you miss her." I lay there, annoyed to think that *this* would be how God would help me. It sure didn't feel like help; it felt like bad advice. Finally, unable to sleep, I grudgingly made a decision that I would do it.

The next day I went to Mary's house, and when she came to the door, I said, through clenched teeth, "I miss you." Mary began to cry. She invited me in, and we talked about our argument. We asked each other's forgiveness—and decided that the makeup business wasn't for us!

I might have waited a long time for Mary to apologize, as she might have waited for me. But in the end an apology wasn't the main thing either of us needed. Mary needed to hear that I missed our friendship, and I needed to take the first step. And I needed to realize that if I listen, God will give me wisdom—even if it doesn't make sense at the time.

Like Calls Out to Like

I need friends—every kind of friend. I need friends who will love me just as I am, hand me a beer when there are no words, kick me in the pants because I need it, or just sit across a table and tell me stories that will make me laugh. I need friends who will send me a book in the mail because it will speak to my heart, friends who will call me to tell me they are on their way to Mass and ask, "How can I pray for you today?" And there are also friends I don't need: friends who are only out to see what they can find wrong with me or to gossip about what is "wrong" with others; friends who only seem to complain or argue or tear down—those are the kinds of friends I don't call friends. And sometimes, I know, I've been that kind of friend myself.

Friendships with women can be difficult. Believe me, I've been a female long enough to know that! Through much of my life, I have often found it easier to be friends with guys. I have some very close male friends whom I would not trade for a moment. I think it mostly has to do with the lack of "drama." But those friendships are different from my friendships with women.

Like calls out to like. My feminine heart hears something different from another feminine heart. And if I am able to see beyond all the drama and competition and fears that I have as a woman, I'm drawn into deeper friendship right from the start.

I've read books over the years about what friendships between women look like, and I've found myself somehow unable to really relate. I probably read the wrong books, but I always felt as if I didn't measure up. I didn't *want* to have a craft party at my house. I didn't *want* to learn how to knit. I *really* didn't want to learn how to scrapbook. I can barely keep my family in clean laundry, and if I have some free time it's going to be on the sofa, hopefully with a freshly delivered pizza and a Diet Coke in hand.

Even if I don't match the women in those books, I do know that friendship is a key piece of my life. God speaks to me through those around me. In a moment like my one with Mary, I hear the voice of God more clearly than ever before.

Takeout was my idea of a home-cooked meal. I had never purchased rosemary, because I had never made a meal that needed it. But I have friends who are amazing cooks and have shared with me some of their simplest recipes. Even *I* can make them work! My root vegetables would make your mouth water. (There was a time when I had no idea what constituted a "root vegetable." Thanks, A.M.C.!) My friends have challenged me to look for opportunities to cook healthier and, honestly, more interesting food for my family.

Along the same lines, my friends have challenged me to read books that will make me think. (Left to my own devices, I tend to go for a mystery or suspense-style book, which is similar to eating a candy bar: It doesn't last long, and it's not very nourishing, but it's enjoyable while I have it.) In the past few years, I've read more books by Henri Nouwen, Mother Teresa, Max Lucado, and other holy men and women than I used to.

Through my friendships I've been challenged to take better care of my body. A friend and I made a commitment to text each other weekly as a way to keep each other accountable to exercise—again, something I would prefer never to do. I'm always a tad envious of those folks who seem to find exercise a joy and can't wait to do it. I wish I had that gene. Both of my sisters do, so it seems really unfair that I missed out on that gift. For far too many years I spent my time not doing anything that could be construed as exercise. At the end of that time, I found myself overweight, without energy, and uninterested in lively activities. That is not how I wanted to live as a wife and mother to three children. So my accountability partner really helps, along with a membership at a gym and a schedule on my fridge to tell me when to go.

All of these are good things, and maybe a guy friend could challenge me to do them, too. But I don't think it would have the same impact. I find that the women in my life have more of a "challenging" impact on me because I'm watching them live out what it means to be a woman.

I'm better for the women in my life—my mother, my sisters, my friends. All of them show me the way to be a woman whose highest hope is that one day, when I meet my Maker, I will hear the words, "Well done, good and faithful servant" (Matthew 25:21). And I will only have to look back over my shoulder to see the many hands that helped hold me steady.

Prison Walls

When I was eight years old, I wrote my first (and last) song. I had a little red plastic guitar with real strings on it. You couldn't tune it, but it was a cool-looking guitar for an eight-year-old. I decided that I was going to be a musician (right after I became a movie star and Miss America and the president).

I will always remember coming into the kitchen and telling my mom that I had written a song and wanted to play it for her. I'm sure she was in the middle of cooking dinner or some other chore, but she obligingly came out to the living room to listen to me. So I hit a few notes (or non-notes) on my guitar and sang this song:

I'm so happy, very full of joy!

I'm so happy, very full of joy!

I feel like I'm way up in the clouds and having fun with the
   sun!

> I feel like I'm holding hands with my God, and we're talking
> about love!

When I was in high school, I came across those words again and wondered what had happened to that eight-year-old girl. Where was the joy? the happiness? the love? The words and emotions that song evoked were nowhere to be found in my life at sixteen. In fact, the poems I had begun writing in high school were all about feeling lonely, unsure, and insecure. I recall two lines in particular:

> I pass through the darkness asking who I am.
> I see the light, it beckons me, I cannot run in sand.

I don't think that I was unique—a lot of us have felt that way at some point. We all have feelings of uncertainty, fear, anxiety, insecurity, and worry.

But what happens in that jump from eight to sixteen, or twenty, or thirty? What takes away that innocent joy and laughter that seemed so natural when we were young?

I think it's a number of things. It can be as simple as the fact that we don't understand that we are still growing and learning. It can also be the fact that life is challenging and downright hard sometimes.

But I am convinced that what happens most often is that we don't see ourselves for who we really are. Too often we look around and see only what is "outside." We assess our ability to be thin enough, stylish enough, successful enough, fabulous enough—these become the things that define who we are. We look in the mirror and wonder, *Do I measure up? Am I normal? Am I enough as I am? If people knew the real me, would they like me? Do I have a place?* We may be able to say that God created us and that he loves us, but to see ourselves as we *really* are is difficult.

I went to prison and saw this in a completely different way.

Lockdown

We've all seen the movies: the clanging doors, the bars on every cell, the hopeless-looking prisoners, the mean-looking guards. The fear. But nothing prepares you for the reality of prison. For going through the metal detectors. For having your valuables, including your car keys, locked up (they are considered a weapon).

I stood there in a cold and barren entryway, palms sweaty, nervous, unsure what to expect. The doors are what really got me. Five large, heavy metal doors that could be opened only by the guard once the ones behind them were closed and locked. Standing between two doors for a few minutes was rather claustrophobic. There were walls everywhere and barbed wire on every wall and door—yes, just as in the movies.

As I entered the common room where I would assist several other women with a Bible study for female inmates, I felt awkward and uncomfortable. I didn't know what to expect or how the women would act (or in all honesty, how *I* would act). Would they be kind or cruel? Would I be comfortable with them or aching to get out of there as quickly as possible?

As the inmates walked into the room, I felt my anxiety increase. I thought to myself, *I have nothing in common with these women. How can I be any help to them? What can I possibly say? Why did I agree to do this?*

As songs of worship were played and the prayer began, I began to relax, and then I got caught up in hearing these women sing and pray. We moved into small groups to discuss the Bible study and allow the women to share any prayer needs.

In my group of eight women, I was struck by the fact that each woman was wearing the exact same outfit: green pants and green shirt (like the scrubs doctors wear) with a yellow T-shirt underneath. (One of my first thoughts, in all honestly, was that yellow is a truly heinous color on almost everybody. Why was that chosen?) Inscribed on the bottoms of their black boots was the word *INMATE*, so that if they escaped, every step they took would leave the markings of an "inmate" on the ground.

Everything about these women screamed out, "Different from me," and it made me uncomfortable. Here was a diverse group of women, representing every race, age, height, weight, eye color, and hair color. Each of them had been put into a green and yellow box with black boots.

One of our greatest expressions of self is our appearance: how we dress and fix our hair, the makeup we wear (or don't wear), and our accessories—jewelry, scarves, hats, purses, and shoes (or the lack thereof). These are things that express us and our own personal style. Rarely do we see someone else wearing exactly what we are wearing! These women had lost the luxury of being distinctive.

Yet I began to see the astounding individual beauty in each of them. And at the same time, I began noticing similarities with me. Their hearts expressed the same things that my heart did. They struggled with loneliness, fear, anger, learning how to love, learning how to forgive, and trying not to gossip. They were learning about a God who loved them as they were but who also called them to become all that he had created them to be. They knew that altering their outward appearance could not make that happen; they recognized that it needed to be an interior change.

As they shared their hearts, I began to appreciate the gifts these women brought to that small group. They didn't have anything external, such as a wardrobe or a career, to show the world how great or how successful they could be. Here, out of sight and on the fringes of society, these women, in the midst of their outward nothingness, were finding their value in God.

One of the women read a Scripture passage from her Bible, which was dog-eared, underlined, and highlighted far more than my own. She shared that her hope is in a God who promises to be with her.

We Are All Failures

Why is our image of ourselves so often tied up in external appearances? We spend so much time and energy on how we look, frequently only bringing upon ourselves more dissatisfaction. We base our worth on how thin we are, how successful we are, or on what a great wife, mother, friend, daughter, sister, or employee we are. When we do that, we will *always* lose. We will never be thin enough, rich enough, smart enough, or successful enough. We will never be able to be a great friend at all times to everyone we love. We will all fail. Peter Pan creator J.M. Barrie wrote, "We are all failures—at least, all the best of us."[1]

Sometimes our failures show us who we really are—or who we don't want to be anymore. Am I unable to deal with conflict? Am I too quick to become angry, hurt, resentful, or self-centered when life is hard or bad things happen? How do I trust that God is present with me, even in the hardest times? How is my whole life a little like being in prison?

Think of the people who have struggled greatly when treated unfairly and cruelly and yet have followed and trusted God through it all. Nelson Mandela comes to mind—a man who spent twenty-seven years in prison (sentenced unfairly) and yet came out of prison ready to forgive those who had put him there. The experience in prison gave him the courage, wisdom, and strength of character that has changed South Africa as he led the nation in unity. But *twenty-seven years* of blind trust? Twenty-seven years of waiting for justice, for change, for freedom?

Mandela often said, "I am the captain of my soul."[2] Therein lies the heart of the matter. We are the ones who choose our reaction to our circumstances. Hear that again: *We choose our reaction.* We may not be able to choose what will happen to us, how we will be treated, what pain may be inflicted upon us—but we do choose our reactions. It's easier said than done, of course, but it's the truth.

I choose my reactions. By the grace of God, I can choose not to allow my circumstances to define me. I have the grace to do that by the working of the Holy Spirit in my life. I can be a woman of courage.

Those women I met in prison chose their reactions to their circumstances. Confined in a place they would rather not be, they looked to God for the grace to get through each day. They spoke about the other women who were incarcerated with them who did not have this hope to grab on to and who spent so much time and energy in anger and fear.

Is there a limit on God's grace? Is there a limit to how far his grace can reach? Nelson Mandela didn't think so. The women in that prison didn't think so, either.

I write to a man in another prison each month to encourage him. His family has written him off. He doesn't know where his daughter is. He doesn't get any mail, not even on his birthday. Each letter I receive from him, every month, mentions something about the darkness in prison. He works hard to be positive, to get through each day, to find grace in every day. His relationship with God, he says, is sometimes the only bright spot in his life. He knows he is responsible to be the captain of his own soul. Am I the captain of mine?

CHAPTER NINE

One Thousand Pounds

My grandmother's house was filled with books. I loved visiting her because I loved to read! The stories and adventures took me away until I couldn't hear anything around me; I would become so engrossed in reading that I often had to be called several times for dinner.

Along with her regular books, Grandma kept a pile of comic books. But these were no ordinary comic books. They were stories of Christian people who had amazing experiences with God. Their stories had been put into comic-book format for kids like me to read and really "get."

I remember the story of a man named Andrew who smuggled Bibles into the Soviet Union. One time the guards stopped him at the border and opened his trunk, which was full of Bibles. Andrew prayed that God would make the men blind, and they slammed the trunk shut and told him to "move along."

These stories captivated me because they were true. I read those comic books until they were frayed at the edges, and much of the print had worn off.

One that I read over and over was the story of Corrie ten Boom.[1] Corrie and her sister, Betsie, lived with their elderly father in Holland during the invasion of the Nazis. They put themselves at tremendous risk by hiding Jews in their home. They built a false wall and practiced an escape plan with the thirty-five fugitives they sheltered.

Corrie was fifty-two years old when the Nazis broke into their home and captured everyone there, including Corrie, her sister, and their father. Harboring Jews was a criminal offense, and they were now treated in the same horrifying manner as the Jews they had sheltered: They were loaded onto cattle cars and sent to a concentration camp. The men were separated from the women, and Corrie never saw her father again.

Corrie and Betsie found themselves in a room with seven women and one blanket. Nights were well below freezing. Food was little more than a thin soup, and the treatment by the guards was violent. Their barracks were filled with despair, illness, lice, hunger, and fear.

Corrie and Betsie began to teach the other women the hymns that they knew by heart. They spent hours reciting the words of Scripture that they had memorized in their years of studying the Bible as a family. The other women found a measure of peace that had not been present in that camp before the ten Boom sisters arrived.

Betsie, who had been frail before coming to the camp, quickly deteriorated in health and died soon after arriving. Corrie found herself overwhelmed with grief and anger at the guards who had treated Betsie with such cruelty when she couldn't keep up with the other workers. She herself received numerous beatings. Yet through it all Corrie continued to recite Scriptures and teach the other women how to find peace and hope outside of their circumstances. Finally, blessedly, Corrie was released from the concentration camp at the end of the war.

She began to travel all over the world sharing her story of hope behind the barbed-wire walls. One night, as she spoke at a church, she saw a tall man in the back of the room. As the evening wore on, she recognized him as one of the cruelest guards from the concentration camp! She found the muscles in her body clench as she relived those horrible months of imprisonment. Anger surged through her as she finished her program.

She was, as always, inundated with people who wanted to talk with her, thank her, share a little bit of their own story with her, ask her to sign their books—making it impossible for her to leave quickly. Out of the corner of her eye, she could see the guard slowly making his way toward her. She looked for a way out of the room, but she was surrounded by the crowd of people trying to reach her. She was trapped.

The man finally made his way to where Corrie stood, trembling, in the middle of the room. He held out his hand as if to shake hers and told her that he had become a Christian. He asked her to forgive him for the cruel ways he had treated both Corrie and her sister.

Corrie's arm felt as if it weighed a thousand pounds as she looked this man in the eye. *This man! The very one who was so cruel to Betsie and me, and now—now—he wants me to forgive him!*

Somehow, with a grace that could come only from God, Corrie was able to lift that thousand-pound arm and place her hand in the man's and tell him, quietly and peacefully, that she did indeed forgive him. The freedom she experienced by saying yes to forgiveness was much more than she expected.

I was only a young girl the first time I read that story, yet even I could see that what Corrie ten Boom had done was nearly miraculous. I asked myself, *Could I do the same? Would I be capable of that kind of forgiveness?* I couldn't imagine. And for many years I didn't have to.

Agony of Defeat

In my professional career in the medical and nonprofit spheres, I had been relatively successful, moving up in position and experience, always feeling that I had a new and better challenge before me. The work was a natural fit with my love of people and my passion for the organizations I worked for.

I went to work for a large national organization and began moving up in the company. I enjoyed what I was doing. In fact, I *loved* what I was doing. I truly thought I had a dream job. Then, in one fell swoop, that was shattered. I found myself sitting in the human resources department being accused of embezzling funds!

The staff had a four-inch binder in front of them with all of my purchases, reimbursements, and credit-card receipts. One by one they went through the pages and asked me to verify what the money was spent on, where I kept the items I purchased, and what I did with them after purchasing them. It was nerve-racking, to say the least, and I found myself stumbling over what to say because I didn't always remember.

One example they brought up was a carton of eggs. Why, they asked me, did I need a carton of eggs? I explained that it was a tool for leadership training: You gave each attendee an egg and asked them to figure out how to make it stand up. Many of the attendees would use cups, stir sticks, or paper to devise some kind of holder for their egg. I would take the egg, crack it gently on the table, and make it stand on its own. The idea was that sometimes the answer is simple and right in front of you.

Now they wanted to know where I kept the eggs after I purchased them and what I did with the eggs when the training was over. It was like that for hours and hours. I had to come back a week later and go through even more interrogation. At the end of that time, they fired me, accusing me of embezzling hundreds of dollars from the organization that I had worked so very hard to raise money for.

They couldn't have accused me of anything worse. I was angry. Hurt. And it only got worse.

As time went on I pursued legal help to protect myself from being sued or slandered. Each time I received paperwork from this organization, the dollar amount that I had supposedly embezzled was increased. The last document I received stated that I had embezzled over ten thousand dollars.

As a trainer for a five-state region, I had spent a lot of money on venues, food, resources, and so on. In fact, ten thousand dollars was the *total* amount I had spent on behalf of the organization during the entire year. In effect they were accusing me of stealing *every single dollar* I had spent while being in their employ over the past year.

My boss, who had approved all of my expenses, was nowhere to be found. I was told she wasn't available to be at any of the meetings. No one advocated for me. I sat in that room by myself with three people on the other side of the table accusing me of things I had never done. I spent many weeks seething in anger and hurt.

I had never had anything like this happen to me before, and I didn't know how to deal with it. I talked it out (I had a six-hundred-dollar phone bill one month to prove it), I walked it out (I lost twenty pounds in three months), I cried it out, and I prayed it out. But in the end I just had to get past it. I had to get, as my dad says, "twenty-five feet in the air above it" to see the truth that was there.

It really wasn't about me. There were all kinds of management issues coming down the pike, and people feared for their jobs. Many of the jobs were to be merged, including mine. Fear helped move decisions along. But no matter what the reasons, I was still hurtfully and wrongfully accused, and I still had to work through that.

I remember speaking at a young-adult event a couple months after this happened and sharing about this situation. Afterward a woman came up to me. She said that she could tell that I wasn't over the hurt yet. I said that I was "trying" to forgive. She looked at me and said, "You have to *choose* to forgive."

Those are words I might have said to another person telling me a story of betrayal and pain. But I needed to hear them that night, because I hadn't yet made that choice. I had to begin to choose to forgive.

I felt like Corrie ten Boom with a thousand-pound arm, except mine was a thousand-pound heart. I felt so angry, so hurt, and so betrayed that I couldn't imagine being able to truly forgive. Henri Nouwen says, "Healing is often so difficult because we don't want to know the pain."[2] I didn't want to really look at it, delve into it, and deal with it. Even now I relive this story as I write it, and I find myself in a bit of a cold sweat as I recall those dark days. It wasn't easy to consider moving past it.

First I chose to stop saying mean things about those involved in the process and the organization as a whole. Then I had to decide if I wanted this to hang over my head (and heart) for the rest of my life. I decided that no, I didn't want that.

Scripture tells us to "take every thought captive" (2 Corinthians 10:5), and that was what I began to do. When angry thoughts began to form in my head, I would stop and purposefully choose not to let my mind go down that path. I didn't always succeed, but I began to succeed more than I failed, and pretty soon those thoughts happened less and less.

I went to confession. I asked forgiveness for any anger I might have harbored against my employers and for any ways that I may have been a poor employee. I didn't want anything hanging over me in any way, so I covered all the bases.

Unexpected Grace

While I would never want to go through something like that experience ever again, it taught me much about God's grace in the midst of difficulty. Life is hard, sometimes because of what we choose and sometimes because of what gets chosen for us. Either way, it is difficult to see past the anger, hurt, betrayal, and pain and believe that there will be a better day.

We need to grieve what we have lost, all the way through, so we can get to the other side. I've watched friends grieve abuse, divorce, addictions, loss of children or parents, unemployment, fear, failure, and betrayal. I know that at times it can feel as if there is no tomorrow and things will never get better. I've been there.

When I was a young girl, my mom and I used to talk about difficult things happening to us. At that point we had never had anything really, really bad happen to either of us. My mom said that when hard things happen to people, they get stronger. I remember laughing and saying that I hoped we could be "wimpy" for the rest of our lives.

But there is no reality in that. The truth is that we all have difficulty and pain, although yours will certainly look different from mine, as "the heart knows its own bitterness" (Proverbs 14:10).

I cannot imagine how Mary, the mother of Jesus, felt when she heard her relatives talk about how crazy Jesus was, or how she must have felt as she followed him to Calvary. She could have chosen to be angry, bitter, or despairing. I'm sure she endured tremendous feelings of grief and pain as she watched him suffer. I often wonder, *Did she know? Had she heard from Jesus, in the quietness of their home, what he was about to do? Or did she, like others, think that he was the king who was going to restore their freedom from the Romans?*

No matter what she believed or knew, I don't know how you would prepare to watch your son beaten and mocked and then crucified. Her ability to be "full of grace" in the midst of such pain is, for me, a comfort in the midst of difficulty.

I find that the things I cannot control are the hardest to let go of. If I have made a poor choice and must pay the consequences, so be it. But when I experience something that I have no control over (like being fired unethically), it is much more difficult. I can look to Mary and her example to give me the courage and grace to let go, forgive, and continue moving forward.

My case wasn't resolved as I would have liked. I ended up having to be satisfied with the court sealing my record. I would have preferred so much more—an apology, their taking responsibility for their actions. But sometimes life just isn't fair, is it? I had to choose to move on.

Often I hear people say, "God has a purpose for everything." I hate that statement. It makes it sound as if he causes everything. I cannot believe that God gives someone cancer or makes accidents happen that cause death and destruction. I cannot believe that God would cause such pain. I do believe, though—because I have experienced this myself and have seen many others experience it—that God will take everything we have and make it into something beautiful—if we let him.

If we let him, God can take even the most horrific circumstances and bring something beautiful out of every one. Beauty from ashes—that is what makes God most holy, most miraculous. But we must *let* him. And when we do, there we find the most amazing grace.

> Amazing grace, how sweet the sound,
> That saved a wretch like me.
> I once was lost, but now am found,
> Was blind but now I see.
>
> —John Newton, 1779

CHAPTER TEN

Chase the Lion[1]

The first book of Chronicles tells an obscure story of a mighty warrior named Benaiah who was considered a great hero. In fact, he went on to become one of King David's most trusted bodyguards. The story says that he chased a lion into a pit and, despite snow and slippery ground, he caught and killed it (see 1 Chronicles 11:22).

What strikes me most about this story is that Benaiah actually *chased* the lion. Most of us, if we saw a running lion, would run in the other direction. We would be supremely grateful that the lion wasn't chasing us! But Benaiah ran *toward* the lion, chasing him all the way into a "no outlet" pit. It was a do-or-die situation when he got down there.

We don't know why he had to catch that lion; maybe it was terrorizing his village, or maybe his family was hungry. It doesn't really matter. What matters is his courage in the midst of an unknown and dangerous situation.

The dictionary tells us that courage is the ability to face pain, fear, or difficulty, that it is a quality of one's mind and spirit. Courage does not mean "I'm not afraid," and it does not mean "I know how things will end." Courage means "I'm willing to take the chance." Courage is expressed by doing what seems scary or makes us feel vulnerable in all kinds of situations.

My daughter Lauren is an amazingly talented artist. Her passion is anime, a Japanese form of cartoon drawing. It is very distinctive and detailed, and Lauren has developed beautiful skills for this work. Other artists and teachers tell her how impressed they are with her artwork. But Lauren needs to be courageous to keep on drawing, trusting that others will appreciate or even admire what she does.

Lauren gave her grandmother a picture for her birthday, and her grandmother framed it and showcased it in her living room. My sister, whose daughter is best friends with Lauren, framed one of Lauren's pictures for her daughter's room. I've framed many of her pictures (but officially I don't really count, because I'm the "not-objective" mom).

Lauren can't see how good she really is, and it's all wrapped up in a fear that others will dislike what is so personal to her. Some of that fear comes out of her actual experience. In an art class not long ago, one of the other students looked at her work and told her that it was OK but probably wouldn't go anywhere because so many others were better. Lauren was absolutely devastated. She told me that she had stopped drawing completely after that because, as she put it, "What's the point? It will never go anywhere."

My heart broke for her. One comment, one hurtful word, and she could easily have lost her ability to see the gift she has and use it as it was intended. It would be easier to put everything in a drawer and not let anyone see it. So I was really proud of her when she allowed our local library to display eight of her pictures for several months. She has chosen to respond to her challenges with courage.

We too are called to live our lives like Benaiah, with the courage that comes from knowing that God walks with us into that pit. Sometimes it just takes stepping out (or running) into something unknown; sometimes it calls for just standing still. I don't want to stand in my own way. I don't want to spend my life being too careful. Have I saved the "good candles" for a special occasion, only to find them melted in the back of the cupboard? Have I held on to a job, a boyfriend, or a friendship that I should move on from? Have I spent all my time waiting, wondering, hoping—for what?

What if you and I started going further than we thought we could? What if we stopped setting little goals that we *know* we can reach and started setting God-sized goals? What if we went after a dream that would definitely fail if God did not intervene?

What if, maybe more than anything else, we stopped trying to be someone we're not? What if we quit running away, quit playing it safe—and started chasing a lion? Even if we couldn't see where it went?

Tangled Up in Rope

While there isn't much of a possibility that any of us will actually need to chase a lion into a pit and kill it (and I find myself grateful for that), we can stop playing it safe. We can chase our own lions. "Chasing a lion" will look different for everyone, because we each are meant to be ourselves and live a life that makes sense for who we are. Take a chance; be yourself; seek God; try a new thing—only *you* can determine what that means in your life.

It might mean making a change that you've been afraid to make. It might mean going back to college or changing your major, breaking up with a boyfriend, digging deep to work on your marriage, spending more time with family or friends, changing jobs, or learning how to do something new.

What I do know is that it will mean doing *something*. In fact, I'm convinced that by standing still we actually begin to go backward. Look at all the areas of your life constantly to be sure that each one is continually challenging you, encouraging you, moving you forward, and inviting you deeper into whom God made you to be.

I'm not giving you permission to leave behind difficult situations (a troubled marriage, for instance) or escape from reality (quitting your job without another plan, for example). But I am encouraging you to take a good, hard look at your life and choose to make some changes.

This doesn't mean that I'm knocking a good evening of popcorn and mindless movies with family or friends either! Sometimes taking the opportunity to relax and enjoy the people around us is just what we need. But sometimes, as I have discovered, that needs to be looked at, too.

A few years ago I found myself living in a rut that I had slipped into without even noticing. It wasn't so much of an external rut, like having the same job or never making new friends; instead it was an internal rut, in which I wasn't doing anything to challenge myself. It was just too easy to come home from work, find another TV show to watch, and spend my evening "relaxing" with the kids. I felt that I worked hard and deserved to relax at the end of the day.

What I didn't see was that I was falling into a kind of laziness. I was losing quality time with my family. I didn't spend enough time looking my children and husband in the eye and hearing how they were doing and what was happening in their lives—both good and bad. And I was losing time with myself.

Other things had stalled in my life as well. I had always wanted to learn to play a musical instrument, but I never took any lessons. I had wanted to lose weight for quite a few years because I wasn't at a healthy weight, but I never made any decisions about it. I had always wanted to write a book, but I never sat down to begin writing.

I finally got to the end of my rope. I found myself out of work for an extended period of time, while in the past I had always been able to find a job fairly easily. I was quickly running out of resources—and out of heart. I felt unsure of my future. I took a long look in the mirror, and I didn't like what I saw. I could see my life unraveling before me, and I didn't want to stay where I was. I wanted—oh, I really wanted!—something new. But I didn't know where to start.

I cried out to God, asking him to "save" me and make everything OK. But God knew better. He knew it was time for me to chase my own lion—to quit holding back and start running into my own pit, even if it looked dark.

In an odd way, my husband started the ball rolling. Our anniversary comes at the end of summer, and this particular year we had decided that, instead of exchanging gifts, we would go out for a nice dinner together (which, with three kids, is not always a possibility!). But on the day before our anniversary, Mark told me that he wanted to give me a gift—a short-term diet program specifically created to give that "shot in the arm" that can really launch someone in a weight-loss program.

I had about fifty pounds to lose and felt overwhelmed with trying to do it myself. Mark knew that. It might seem like an odd anniversary gift, and some people might even say he was insensitive for giving me a diet as a present. But I think it is one of the most beautiful gifts he has ever given me. He saw that I was floundering and needed a "win." I needed to see that I was capable of something that was hard to do. And so I started. (Well, I started right after that aforementioned anniversary dinner!)

Now I look back in amazement. I'm forty pounds lighter (and still working on that last ten, which, as everyone says, is the hardest); I began to take ukulele lessons (although my sister says it's the dorkiest instrument I could choose); and as you can see from the book in your hands, I have actually finished writing a book. Not only that, but I finally found a job that fits me well and brings me joy and energy. That first "win" pushed me into so many more.

Sometimes getting to the end of your rope is just what you need. I'm not saying it feels good or that I'd love to go back there. But getting to that point made me take a hard look at my life, and it made me push for something better. Perhaps if I had just stayed where I was, I wouldn't be writing these words now. Maybe I would be on cholesterol medication because I didn't take care of my body. Maybe I would be OK, or maybe not. But to live in a rut of your own doing or to live in fear is no way to live at all. Instead of spending the rest of my life wondering if I had missed something better that I just didn't walk far enough to see, I learned something about trust that I had never understood before.

While I was out of work, many people would tell me to "just trust God." After a while I wanted to scream out, "Easy for you to say; you have a job!" But what does trust really mean? Does it mean that everything will work out perfectly?

What about those people in Haiti who put their children to bed hungry most nights and yet have faith that puts many others', including my own, to shame? What about those in our very own communities who live in abject poverty yet experience a peace "which passes all understanding" (Philippians 4:7)?

I began to see that trust means believing that no matter what I will have to walk through, God will be with me, and I will be OK. Bad things will still happen. Trusting God isn't a ticket to a life of ease. Trusting God means that we live with hope, encouragement, and expectation. Hear these words; read them aloud:

Let us hold fast the confession of our hope without wavering, for *he who promised is faithful.* (Hebrews 10:23, emphasis mine)

The virtue of hope…keeps man from discouragement, it sustains him during times of abandonment, it opens up his heart in expectation. (*CCC*, #1818)

At the beginning of the Gospel of Matthew, we read that Jesus was called "Emmanuel," meaning "God with us" (Matthew 1:23). At the end of that same Gospel, Jesus tells us that he will be with us always (Matthew 28:20). These Scriptures speak truth to our hearts. Each time I kneel before the altar in worship of the One who made me and promised to be with me always, and who shares his very Body and Blood with me, I am living in trust. I can trust that he is with me no matter what happens.

Even though this journey will not be perfect, it is up to us to walk it in faith and hope. As I have shared with you, I do know what it is to be afraid—to wonder if tomorrow will be better than today, or just the same, or maybe worse. Whether we experience victory or failure, the key is trusting that through it all he is with us. God with us: Emmanuel.

It's time to stop playing it safe and start taking risks. Worry less about what people think and more about what God thinks. Don't try to be who you're not. Be yourself. Laugh at yourself. Quit holding out. Quit holding back. Quit running away. Chase the lion.

A Journey of Threads

I once heard a story of a woman who was working on a tapestry. Her small child sat at her feet every day and played while she sewed. One day the child looked up at his mother and asked her why she was sewing such a mess of thread. The mother invited him to come and sit on her lap to see the top. When the child looked at the top of the tapestry, he gasped with delight as he saw a beautiful picture of a garden filled with brightly colored flowers.

Just like this child, we often aren't able to see the whole picture, the whole tapestry. Only God can see the entire panorama, the development of our lives, a journey of threads, each one helping to make up one final masterpiece that takes an entire lifetime to create.

Think about it. Each of the threads of our lives has a purpose and offers a particular kind of beauty. Each strand carries importance to the final picture. In my own tapestry I would expect to see bright colors and sparkly threads dominate. (If they make a glittery pink and silver thread, I'm pretty sure that would be me.) I never thought about the other colors that are necessary to make the silver stand out and shine. I never thought about black.

It would have served me well to know that the black threads of life are necessary to offset the colored threads. Silver, gold, yellow, green, and blue are striking against a dark background. But in the midst of a time that seems to be woven of nothing but black thread, it is hard to see the bigger picture. Imagine—when Benaiah entered that pit to find that lion, he dove straight into blackness.

When black threads seem to make up the *entire* tapestry of your life, all you can see are the things you don't like. I've been there. I once spent two long years looking at nothing but black threads, in fact.

For twelve years, I had lived in a small, close-knit community and had taken for granted all the friendships and support. When we moved to another part of the country, I assumed that things would be about the same in the new place. We would get involved in the church, make friends, and reestablish a sense of community. But it wasn't like that. My job, the loneliness of living in a new place, the culture of the church we were involved in—I just couldn't see anything I liked.

I spent most of the two years that I lived there wishing for something else. I missed my friends, my house, my church, my favorite restaurants—even my hairdresser. I spent far too much time wishing for the same "colored threads" as I had before.

What was I thinking? This was a new place, a different sort of community. Instead of wasting my energy in regrets, wishing I could recapture what I had lost, I should have challenged myself to reach out and try something new.

I guess I was still thinking in pink silvery thread or "princess" mode. As a little girl, I saw and loved all the Disney movies. But here's the reality: We don't live in a fairy tale, and there are no fairy godmothers to change our pumpkins into carriages and our rags into ball gowns. Life is imperfect, filled with black threads that weave through our lives and cause pain and hurt and struggle.

We do have someone better than a fairy godmother, however: a God who is bigger than anything we will walk through, bigger than the biggest pain of our heart, and bigger than the greatest joy you could imagine. (And to be honest, I think that Sleeping Beauty probably became addicted to sleeping pills, and Prince Charming left Snow White for someone younger and with a more *normal* voice.)

Fairy tales aren't real, but we have a book filled with promises that will be kept by the God who made us. Over and over Scripture speaks words of truth to our hearts:

> But now thus says the LORD, he who created you,
> …
>   he who formed you…:
> "Fear not, for I have redeemed you;
>   I have called you by name, you are mine." (Isaiah 43:1)

> I have loved you with an everlasting love;
>   therefore I have continued my faithfulness to you.
> (Jeremiah 31:3)

> Have no anxiety about anything, but in everything by prayer and supplication with thanksgiving let your requests be known to God. And the peace of God, which passes all understanding, will keep your hearts and your minds in Christ Jesus. (Philippians 4:6–7)

> For we are his workmanship, created in Christ Jesus for good works. (Ephesians 2:10)

When we grab these truths spoken by and about the God who made us and loves us more than we can imagine, the core of our being is renewed. They remind us of the truth that was placed in us at our very creation!

You and I were made by a God who formed us from the beginning, called us by name, and knows our hearts! "God is greater than our hearts, and he knows everything" (1 John 3:20). No longer do we see difficulties as defeating; we see them as challenges and opportunities to grow and learn. No longer do we run away from pain; we look it straight in the eye and listen to the words it speaks. No longer do we fear—for "there is no fear in love" (1 John 4:18).

We have met Love.

> So promise me you'll never forget…that you aren't an accident, or an incident… You are a gift to the world, a divine work of art, signed by God. You were deliberately planned, specifically gifted, and lovingly positioned on this earth… by the Master Craftsman.
>
> —Max Lucado, *God Thinks You're Wonderful*[2]

Things I've Learned

It's hard to know how to end a book. It feels as if there is still so much unsaid, so many words not shared.

I've been around the block, so to speak, a few times. And I've learned some things—some good, some bad, and some just fun. But that's what life is about: a journey of joy, sorrow, and hopefully a lot of laughter. Here's a list of twenty-five things I'll leave you with.

1. While I know it isn't necessary, at 5:00 AM I am really glad I'm a woman. One word: concealer.
2. Sometimes a new lipstick *really does* make everything better.
3. Henri J. Nouwen, Maya Angelou, Max Lucado, C.S. Lewis, and St. Augustine are writers that never fail to speak to my heart.
4. Paint can change a whole room—for not much money (even for me, someone who doesn't like to paint).
5. Some styles should *never* come back: mullets, hammer pants, and leg warmers (to name just a few).

6. Liking fashion or makeup doesn't make you shallow or selfish. It's one of the wonderful ways you have of celebrating you.

7. It's not ridiculous to own several pairs of black shoes, no matter what your husband says.

8. Reading a suspense novel isn't a "waste" of time any more than enjoying a bowl of ice cream is a waste. Neither lasts long, but they are enjoyable.

9. Sometimes wearing a tiara is OK.

10. While it may seem old-fashioned, I believe you learn a lot about a woman by her shoes and handbag (or lack thereof).

11. The Gospel of John is my favorite—written by Jesus' best friend (and isn't that whom you'd want to hear about Jesus from)?

12. Red nail polish will always be classy.

13. A hero isn't someone who can leap tall buildings; a hero is someone who has an autistic child and fights for him. My sister Joleen is my hero.

14. A hero isn't someone famous; a hero is someone who walks away from a life of brokenness and despair and finds freedom and joy. Laura is my hero.

15. A hero isn't someone who can fly; a hero is a woman who chooses to leap when she can't see what's ahead and builds her wings on the way down. Be your own hero.

16. A hero isn't someone who can make everything better; a hero is someone who can make it better for one person. Mother Teresa is my hero.

17. Sparkle—whether it be glitter or Swarovski crystals—brings joy.

18. Facebook and Twitter, while fun ways to find out inane things about each other, can never replace personal conversations.

19. Don't ever settle. A boy who lies will probably always lie. (Lesson #1 of ninth grade.) Never settle for less than what you deserve.

20. There has never been a time that Isaiah 43 did not speak to my heart.

21. Laugh out loud every day. Hopefully more than once a day.

22. Have one friend, one *really good* friend, that you talk with every week.

23. Every day, think of three things you are grateful for and say them out loud.

24. As often as possible, try something new—maybe even something you are afraid of.

25. And last, but most important, every day, in every moment, remember that you—yes, you—are an amazing wonder of God's creation—the crowning achievement of all God created.

> If you ask me what I came to do in this world…,
> I will answer you: I am here to live out loud!
>
> —Emile Zola[1]

Introduction

1. Catherine of Siena, *Letter* 368, as quoted by John Paul II, Homily for the Closing of World Youth Day, no. 7, August 20, 2000, www.vatican.va (accessed May 4, 2011).

Chapter One: A Love Story

1. Pope John Paul II, *The Genius of Women* (Washington, D.C.: USCCB, 1997), p. 27.

2. The *Merriam-Webster* dictionary defines feminism as "the theory of the political, economic, and social equality of the sexes; organized activity on behalf of women's rights and interests."

3. Pope John Paul II, "The Genius of Women," in *The Angelus Reflections, 1995*, ed. David O. Brown (Washington, D.C.: United States Catholic Conference, 1997), pp. 22–23. Two other quotes:

   Without the contribution of women, society is less alive, culture impoverished, and peace less stable. Situations where women are prevented from developing their full potential and from offering the wealth of their gifts should therefore be considered profoundly unjust, not only to women themselves but to society as a whole (p. 27).

This original biblical message is fully expressed in Jesus' words and deeds. In his time women were weighed down by an inherited mentality in which they were deeply discriminated. The Lord's attitude was a "consistent protest against whatever offends the dignity of women" (*Mulieris Dignitatem*, no. 15). Indeed he established a relationship with women which was distinguished by great freedom and friendship (pp. 22–23).

4. Joseph Nowinsk, *The Tender Heart: Conquering Your Insecurity* (New York: Fireside, 2001), p. 23.

5. Naomi Wolf, *The Beauty Myth* (New York: HarperCollins, 2002), p. 10.

6. Beth Moore, *So Long, Insecurity* (Carol Stream, Ill.: Tyndale, 2010), p. 42.

Chapter Two: Crown of Creation

1. See, for example, Pope John Paul II, *Dies Domini*, Apostolic Letter on Keeping the Lord's Day Holy, no. 11, May 31, 1998: "It speaks, as it were, of God's lingering before the 'very good' work (*Gn* 1:31) which his hand has wrought, in order to cast upon it *a gaze full of joyous delight*. This is a 'contemplative' gaze which does not look to new accomplishments but enjoys the

beauty of what has already been achieved. It is a gaze which God casts upon all things, but in a special way upon man, the crown of creation."

2. Carol Kelly-Gangi, ed., *Mother Teresa, Her Essential Wisdom* (New York: Fall River, 2006), p. 110.

Chapter Five: Falling Off the Wall

1. *Shadowlands* (Price Entertainment, 1993), quoted at www.imdb .com (accessed May 4, 2011).

2. Henri Nouwen, *Life of the Beloved* (New York: Crossroad, 1992), p. 58.

Chapter Six: How Bad Do You Want It?

1. See Aron Ralston, *Between a Rock and a Hard Place* (London: Simon and Schuster, 2004); *127 Hours* (Cloud Eight Films, 2010).

Chapter Seven: The Best Kind of Friendship

1. Nouwen, *Life of the Beloved,* p. 65.

2. Henri J.M. Nouwen, *Bread for the Journey: A Daybook of Wisdom and Faith* (New York: HarperCollins, 1997), entry for May 2.

Chapter Eight: Prison Walls

1. J.M. Barrie, *Courage* (New York: Charles Scribner's Sons, 1922), p. 26.

2. "I am the captain of my soul" is the last line of the poem *Invictus* by William Ernest Henley (1849–1903). Mandela is reported to have recited the poem for his fellow prisoners at Robben Island.

Chapter Nine: One Thousand Pounds

1. You can read Corrie ten Boom's entire story in *The Hiding Place* (New York: Bantam, 1984).

2. Nouwen, *Life of the Beloved,* p. 93.

Chapter Ten: Chase the Lion

1. This chapter was inspired by Mark Batterson, *In a Pit with a Lion on a Snowy Day: How to Survive and Thrive When Opportunity Roars* (Colorado Springs: Multnomah, 2006).

2. Max Lucado, *God Thinks You're Wonderful!* (New York: MJF, 2003), pp. 58, 69, 66, 68.

Chapter Eleven: Things I've Learned

1. Emile Zola, as quoted at http://readcentral.com (accessed May 4, 2011).

About the Author

TAMMY EVEVARD is a nationally recognized motivational speaker, consultant, and trainer. For nearly two decades, Tammy has been presenting inspiring programs on topics such as youth leadership, womanhood, team-building, and faith development. She is passionate about the love of God and the inherent dignity each person brings to the world. Tammy has been featured on CNN and EWTN and is a regular speaker at national youth conferences.